The Power of Gratitude

Gordon Ferguson

The Power of Gratitude

DPI
DISCIPLESHIP
PUBLICATIONS
INTERNATIONAL

The Power of Gratitude
©1999 by Discipleship Publications International
One Merrill Street, Woburn, MA 01801

Printed in the United States of America

Cover design: Ladislao Mandiola and Chad Crossland
Interior design: Chad Crossland
Cover Image ©1999 PhotoDisc

ISBN: 1-57782-124-6

To the Paris Church of Christ: the ministry staff, the office staff, all other leaders and every member of this special group who are all now deeply embedded in our hearts. The first half of 1999 that Theresa and I were able to spend in your presence will forever be one of our most cherished memories. May God bless you for showering your love on us so abundantly. We are highly honored and deeply humbled to be viewed as your spiritual mom and dad.

Contents

Acknowledgments

Writing this part of a book's introductory material is to me a huge challenge. My memory is not strong enough, my mind not insightful enough and my heart not pure enough to recognize all of the influences God has used to enable me to write the books I have been privileged to write.

Besides Christ, my loving wife, Theresa, contributes more to what I am able to do than anyone else. Only the Lord knows how she so cheerfully lives with my schedule and my moods. Surely God has a special place in heaven reserved for her!

My children and their mates conjure up feelings of gratitude in my heart on a daily basis. I am so proud of who they are and what they do as disciples of Jesus. I am overwhelmed by their grace toward me, a dad who often feels as a parent that he was "too soon old and too late smart."

Randy and Kay McKean, along with their leadership group in the New England/Continental Europe world sector, offer me much encouragement as a writer and teacher. Larger churches now exist in the movement, but the Boston church has been and still is a most special place. Serving as an elder and teacher here is a blessing beyond my ability to comprehend. Serving alongside my fellow elder and friend, Wyndham Shaw, along with his wife, Jeanie, is a rich blessing and an upward call.

Tom and Sheila Jones continue to be among our very best friends, as well as editors par excellence. Tom's knowledge of the Bible, the movement and human nature makes him absolutely irreplaceable. His editing guidance relieves my worries about the material that is published with my name on it, knowing that he will sharpen its quality of communication and protect its contents from serious error. The others whose trained eyes also carefully scan and improve it are heroes to me: Kim Hanson, Lisa Morris, Amy Morgan (a professional proofreader who lives in Buffalo, New York) and sometimes Jerri Newman.

Above all, God is to be thanked and praised for using the likes of me to do his bidding. He has given me the gifts of teaching and writing, along with the opportunities to develop them. And he often uses them even when I am not at my best emotionally and spiritually. As the example of the Corinthian church well illustrates, possessing and using God's gifts does not thereby demonstrate the spirituality of the ones thus endowed! Being keenly aware of both this principle and my own deficiencies, I freely acknowledge once more the overwhelming grace of a God whose love is beyond my feeble grasp. May he once again be able to accomplish good from my efforts to honor him and to point others toward him through the written word.

How Soon We Forget

*F*ew sins are as disgusting as ingratitude. A study of God's dealings with mankind would surely demonstrate how strongly God thinks that this is indeed the case. We humans agree with his assessment—as long as we are observing a lack of thankfulness in the lives of others! However, we often appear fairly unaware of the depth of this problem in ourselves. If we can learn to see through God's eyes, hopefully we can be moved to a consistent repentance of this sin of ingratitude.

The fatal plunge of the first century world into degradation and perversion began with a loss of thankfulness toward God. Romans 1:21 makes this genesis of a downward spiral into disaster very clear: "For although they knew God, they neither glorified him as God nor gave thanks to him, but their thinking became futile and their foolish hearts were darkened." I have not written a book on gratitude simply because this quality makes us happier people or better people; I have written it because a scarcity of gratitude will most surely lead to our missing heaven. Our failure generally to appreciate the magnitude of the subject's importance demonstrates just how effective Satan has been in deceiving us. Had our mother Eve not lost her appreciation for God and his wondrous grace, she would not have taken the fatal bite of forbidden fruit. Let's not underestimate for a moment the vital nature of the study of this topic. It is paramount to our eternal destiny.

Why do we lose our gratitude so easily? Several reasons come to mind rather quickly. One, we often have a shallow grasp of our own sinfulness. A good study of Romans 1-3 should help us deepen our convictions about the magnitude of our sin. Here, Paul is the Spirit's tool to convict us of sin, righteousness and judgment (John 16:7-8). When I teach on these three chapters, I entitle them "The Best of Us Is a Mess." And we really are a mess in comparison to Jesus Christ. However, we all too often measure ourselves by other people which makes us feel reasonably righteous in comparison. The more we see Jesus as he is and ourselves as we are, the more we are going to be grateful that God has reached down in mercy to such undeserving creatures.

Two, we are plagued with abysmally short memories. In 2 Peter 1, the apostle reminds us that a real understanding of God's grace should move us to be growing continually. Peter views a failure to respond in this way as quite unnatural, no matter how common it may be: "he is nearsighted and blind, and has forgotten that he has been cleansed from his past sins" (2 Peter 1:9). The old adage "familiarity breeds contempt" is often true, even when the familiarity is with our Creator.

Three, ingratitude may simply trace back to a sinful heart that blocks the understanding—and therefore the appreciation—of spiritual realities. I remember times when I dealt with sin in my heart in a radical way (which for me means with much prayer, often accompanied by fasting). After such times my spiritual heart seems soft and sensitive, and the tears of appreciation flow easily. Thinking back to those moving experiences makes me marvel at how quickly the tenderness of heart can fade.

Four, a self-focused life certainly results in little thankfulness. My childhood years contributed to my self-focus. Although I was raised in a very blue-collar setting, without an abundance of money, we were comfortable, and I was given much of what I requested. In less kindly terms, I was *spoiled* (hopefully not permanently!). As a result, I characteristically respond to events in my life in a selfish way. When things go well for me, I think, *Fine, that's the way it should be.* When things don't go well for me, I react internally by thinking, *What is going on here? I am Gordon B. Ferguson, Jr. This shouldn't be happening to me!* When I allow my sinful nature to lead me in this direction, I respond to blessings without much thankfulness and to challenges without much grace. Prayerfully, I have made lots of progress in changing these tendencies, but I must guard against them continually to avoid being an ingrate.

Five, a suspect picture of God is one of the more serious, yet subtle, culprits behind ingratitude. We develop our view of God from the most important authority figures in our lives, normally our fathers. If our fathers were beneficent, leaning toward permissiveness with us, we are likely to take God's goodness for granted. If our fathers were distant or harsh, we are likely to view God in much the same way. And if we see him as impersonal, uncaring or demanding, we will misinterpret life's blessings and challenges, remaining unaware of the bounty of his grace. The reality of who he is and what he does can be missed almost entirely. If we are like the one-talent man in Matthew 25, we will see him as a "hard" man (verse 24). If we are like the older brother in the Parable of the Lost Son, we will see him as a father who has done absolutely nothing for us (Luke 15:29). *Astounding!*

For everyone who decides to seek Jesus seriously, a study of the book of Romans is a must. When we begin to understand the God it portrays, we can be consistently motivated by gratefulness for his amazing grace.

Whatever the cause of ingratitude, the cure is in taking the time to figure out life as God designed it to be, rather than life as Satan wants us to see it. Then the message will not be how soon we forget, but how often and deeply we remember the overwhelming goodness of our God.

Hopefully the following brief chapters will bring to mind the simple truths and profound blessings insepara- bly linked to gratitude. I have made no attempt to cover the subject in any sort of systematic manner, or to try to treat it fully. But prayerfully, the following thoughts will provide some very helpful insights to keep you growing. To that end I write. Enjoy!

1

Trees, Clap Your Hands

The mountains and hills
    will burst into song before you,
and all the trees of the field
    will clap their hands.

Isaiah 55:12

*T*he fishing had been good that late, humid Louisiana afternoon. I had caught about ten largemouth bass, and their pungent smell, which was now all over my hands and jeans, was suspended in the stillness of the air. But, smelly or not, I was a very happy fifteen-year-old. The fish had quit biting about as suddenly as they had started, and I was sitting on the ground in a thick mat of pine needles, leaning up against the large tree that produced them. I looked across the pond to the meadow beyond, on past it to the tall rows of corn gently waving in the slight breeze, and in the distance, to the forests. To an outdoorsy kid, it was a breathtaking sight.

Then I did something which was very unusual for me at that point in my life—I prayed and thanked God for his creation. I wasn't at all spiritually minded, but I prayed nonetheless. I couldn't help it! The trees were clapping their hands, the hills were singing, the heavens and earth were rejoicing, and I had to join in. If you are familiar with Old Testament poetic terminology, such analogies from nature are not surprising to you. Read these stirring examples:

> The meadows are covered with flocks
>> and the valleys are mantled with grain;
>> they shout for joy and sing. (Psalm 65:13)

> Let the heavens rejoice, let the earth be glad;
>> let the sea resound, and all that is in it;
>> let the fields be jubilant, and everything in them.
> Then all the trees of the forest will sing for joy.
> (Psalm 96:11-12)

> Let the sea resound, and everything in it,
>> the world, and all who live in it.
> Let the rivers clap their hands,
>> let the mountains sing together for joy.
> (Psalm 98:7-8)

> Praise him, you highest heavens
>> and you waters above the skies.
> Let them praise the name of the Lord,
>> for he commanded and they were created...
> Praise the Lord from the earth,
>> you great sea creatures and all ocean depths,
> lightning and hail, snow and clouds,
>> stormy winds that do his bidding,
> you mountains and all hills,
>> fruit trees and all cedars,
> wild animals and all cattle,
>> small creatures and flying birds.
> (Psalm 148:4-5, 7-10)

God's physical creation bands together in praising him, and it bids us to join in the thanksgiving chorus! Did you ever stop to think that the human creation is the only part of creation that does not function according to design? The rest of creation, animate and inanimate, honors God by doing exactly what they (or *it*) are designed to do. Cows and birds do a far better job of praising God than most humans, simply by the fact that they function the way God wants them to function. Only we humans, with our amazing freedom of choice, mess it up. Outperformed by a cow, by a pig, by a lizard—what a thought! But for most human beings, it is true. Let's make sure that we are not among those who fail to operate according to God's plan.

As I write this, I am looking out over a small lake from the window of a little hotel near Paris. We have been in France for several months working with the church in Paris and helping in various ways with the European mission. At the advice of my editor I am spending five days in isolation to concentrate solely on writing. The lake is filled with fish and waterfowl, and the woods surrounding it with wildlife. I have never heard such noisy nocturnal sounds in my life, nor have I heard some of these particular sounds. At first, I assumed the noise was coming from some kind of raucous birds, but then another hotel guest informed me that the locals attribute the sounds to frogs who are at the height of mating season. During the day, they are pretty quiet. However, at nightfall they kick into full gear and make some of the loudest, strangest sounds you can imagine. Last night was my first night here, and their chorus lasted until well past midnight. Hopefully I will sleep through it all a bit better tonight! But I love it, because I know God loves it. They are doing exactly what he designed them to do—praise him, and praise him *loudly*.

My computer program shows 243 references in the Bible with the word "praise." Add the words "praised," "praising" and "praises," and the count increases by seventy-five. Clearly, God intends for his creation, especially those made in his image, to praise him abundantly. Ephesians 1 speaks of our praising God, his grace and his glory (verses 3, 6, 12, 14). Why is it so important to him that we prolifically praise him? For starters, just because it is right. But since he is absolutely selfless, it has to be because *we* need it.

Sometimes we talk about using the acrostic "ACTS" as a guide for our prayers. The *A* stands for adoration, the *C* for confession of sins, the *T* for thanksgiving and the *S* for supplication (asking God for what we need, or *think* we need). Two of the four are aimed at praising God, which is good, but are we following such a pattern in our prayer times?

I know that the technique is just that, a technique, but who can argue Biblically with the focus of having at least half of our prayer times directed toward the praise of God? As an emotionally based person, I know that a part of my time needs to include casting all of my anxiety on him (1 Peter 5:7, Philippians 4:6-7). But if I am just unburdening myself emotionally, where is the praise for him? Emotionally based or not, all of us need much more of a focus on adoring and thanking God in our prayers. It does something for us that we must have if we are to become like Jesus and represent him before others effectively.

Perhaps you do not know how to pray longer prayers that praise, adore and thank God. Surely God has helped meet this need with the inclusion of 150 psalms in Scripture. They are a record of prayers and songs offered up to God by a number of different people (mostly by David), and they provide examples of just about any kind of possible prayer. Plenty of people have categorized them into different types, including me, but I think all of us need to do that for ourselves. Private worship has much to do with personal preferences, and going through the process of deciding how these psalms speak to your heart will strike many melodious chords in the depths of your soul. Take the time to do such a study. You will be richly rewarded.

Prayers of adoration and thanksgiving are found all through the book of Psalms, and they can serve as a very effective guide for these types of prayers. To help you get started, read and pray through Psalms 8, 24, 29, 47, 92, 93, 95, 96, 98, 100, 104, 113, 135, 147 and 148. Read a verse or two at a time, and then elaborate in your own words the sentiment of the psalmist's wording. Praying the Scriptures is a tremendous way to pray generally, and praying the book of Psalms is my favorite part of such praying. Praying in this way for at least half of your daily prayer times will revolutionize your prayer life. Try it—you'll like it—and you can be sure that God will appreciate it!

Lately, I have been trying to visualize myself pouring out God's love to others. When I am loving them, I want them to feel that he is loving them through me. He promised to pour out his love into our hearts through the Holy Spirit (Romans 5:5), and surely he does this in order that we might then share what he has given us with others. But how does he pour out his love? I think he pours it out only as we learn to focus on it, to feel it, to deeply desire it and to want to share it with others for the express purpose that he might be praised by more and more people.

The more we talk about something, the more it becomes a reality to us. This is why praising God is so vital. It is only when we recount his love and mercy repeatedly that it seems real in our hearts and lives. We have been blessed by him in order to share our blessings with those who are as yet unblessed with salvation. Paul described it this way in 2 Corinthians 4:15: "All this is for your benefit, so that the grace that is reaching more and more people may cause thanksgiving to overflow to the glory of God."

We were created for the praise of his glory, and then recreated for the praise of his glory. The trees, the rivers, the mountains and yes, the cows and lizards, are all far ahead of us in this business of praising our Creator. Let's make some firm decisions about our prayer lives in focus, content and time spent. Then we can join in the resounding chorus with the rest of creation as we function according to design.

> Let the sea resound, and everything in it,
>   the world, and all who live in it.
> Let the rivers clap their hands,
>   let the mountains sing together for joy.
> (Psalm 98:7-8)

Growing in Gratitude

In your average prayer time, what percentage of it do you think you spend giving thanks?

Will you commit to praying carefully through each of the psalms mentioned in this chapter over the next week, spending at least one-third of your prayer time doing this?

Identify and memorize a new favorite "praise" verse. Try to remember it when you are tempted to be discouraged.

2

Badly Out of Focus

> So Ahab went home, sullen and angry because Naboth the Jezreelite had said, "I will not give you the inheritance of my fathers." He lay on his bed sulking and refused to eat.
>
> 1 Kings 21:4

*H*ave you ever noticed children who were happily playing until they noticed the one toy that they didn't have being played with by another child? Suddenly their joy fades, and they become totally focused on the toy that the other kid has. They probably have dozens of better toys, but their selfish natures kick into high gear when their focus is off kilter. Of course, none of us adults would ever be guilty of forgetting dozens of blessings while we rue the lack of the one other blessing which is not ours! King Ahab of the Old Testament was a man whose selfish, greedy character will convict us of the sin of ingratitude.

Ahab, the seventh king of Israel during the period of the divided kingdom, was a self-serving man. His selfishness evidenced itself in many ways, including his marriage to Jezebel, the wicked worshiper of foreign gods. No greater example of his self-serving heart can be found than in his encounter with Naboth.

The story is recorded in 1 Kings 21. Naboth, although a poor man, owned a little vineyard near the palace of Ahab. In spite of his vast holdings, Ahab felt that he just had to own this little vineyard, for it would be a convenient place in which to raise his vegetables. The problem was that Naboth had received the vineyard as an inheritance, and God's decree was that the families retain such inheritances for their future generations to use. For Naboth, it was a matter of divine principle, so he turned down the king's offer to purchase it from him.

Ahab went home so filled with anger that he lost his appetite and lay sulking on his bed, acting just like a spoiled little kid. His wife came in and found him in this condition and taunted him a bit: "What's the matter, big boy? Someone steal one of your toys?" He whined out the story about not being able to have what he wanted, and Jezebel hatched up the devilish plot to falsely accuse Naboth and have him killed. Not only did they have him falsely accused and murdered, they also had his sons killed in order to prevent any heir from trying to reclaim the property later. No wonder God's estimation of him was so bleak: "There was never a man like Ahab, who sold himself to do evil in the eyes of the Lord, urged on by Jezebel his wife" (1 Kings 21:25).

Gratitude and ingratitude are both totally based on our focus in life. Be sure of this: Whatever we focus on is what will seem true for us. If we focus on the flaws of any person, we will soon just see the flaws when we look at them. If we only concentrate on what is displeasing about a situation, it will seem to be a very bad situation. My wife is a wonderfully spiritual woman. She has many, many pluses. On the other hand, she is not perfect. Most of the time, I focus on her many great qualities, and I am very grateful for her and for the thirty-four years that we have been husband and wife. Occasionally, I find myself being critical of her, focusing on her imperfections (as if I had none). At that point, I either quickly repent, or I end up hurting her—and hurting myself as well. It is without question simply a matter of focus. Focus on the positives in life, and you will be filled with gratitude. Focus on the negatives, and you will be an ingrate. It is just as simple as that.

I remember a minister's wife in my former denomination who always seemed to be focused on the negatives. For her, there was never a silver lining to any cloud. She expected the worst and often received it (at least in her distorted mind). A friend of mine was one of her relatives and knew her very well. He said this of her: "Well, one thing is for sure—she will never be disappointed!" Perhaps that was her problem. Maybe her early life had been filled with many disappointments, so she had figured out a way to avoid being let down by assuming the worst all the time. However, if we adopt this approach, life itself will be one big disappointment, as it seemed to be for her.

How about you? Are you often characterized by negative thinking? Do you assume the best or the worst about people and situations? Is your glass half full or half empty? How do you handle disappointments, even little ones? How do you handle interruptions and other minor irritants? Someone once said that you can tell the size of the person by the size of the things it takes to make him angry. How big a person are you?

I was once trying to help a young Christian who was perennially struggling spiritually. He definitely had a negative bent of mind. Suspecting that it took some bad training to produce this in him, I asked him to describe his father. (The parent of the same sex often has the most influence on how our characters are developed.) He said that his dad's favorite expression was, "This is a pain in the neck." No matter the size of the problem, it was magnified into a pain in the neck. His father (and now he) always went around ticked off at the "difficulty" of one thing after another. What a way to live!

As Paul concluded a section in Philippians 4 about overcoming anxiety and being thankful, he gave this admonition:

> Finally, brothers, whatever is true, whatever is noble,
> whatever is right, whatever is pure, whatever is lovely,
> whatever is admirable—if anything is excellent or
> praiseworthy—think about such things. (Philippians 4:8)

All of us have good things in our lives and all of us have not-so-good things in our lives. We have to make a choice about which will permeate our thinking and characterize our hearts. When someone asks how our lives are going, we don't say, "Good/bad." We make a choice one way or the other. When we are asked how we are feeling, we don't say, "Happy/sad." We make a choice. Paul tells us to focus on all that is good and noble, rather than on the things that we wish were different.

"Yes, Paul, but what about...?"

"No, no," he would say. "Don't think about those things; think about the things on my list!" At the time he wrote those words, he was in chains as a prisoner (Philippians 1:17). Of all people, he was certainly not unacquainted with challenges in life. But he had learned how to focus spiritually:

> I know what it is to be in need, and I know what it is
> to have plenty. I have learned the secret of being
> content in any and every situation, whether well fed
> or hungry, whether living in plenty or in want. I can
> do everything through him who gives me strength.
> (Philippians 4:12-13)

We all have things about ourselves and our situations that we can wish were different. (Yes, of course, change the things that can be changed.) In fact, we probably would like to have something different about almost everything, for this life is not characterized by perfection. But in the process of focusing on what we wish were different, we often lose the joy of all that is good. When our thought processes frequently include "what if..." or "if only...," we are not going to be the kind of person who will attract others to Jesus.

Being content is a decision, as is being happy generally. Visiting extremely poor segments of the population of some third world countries and watching the children at play convinces me that life's circumstances are not the greatest determining factor in happiness; it is our focus. These little guys may be naked and have only sticks to play with, but they are laughing and having fun. Jesus said that we must become like little children in order to go to heaven (Matthew 18:3), which means that we have to decide that life is good in spite of the bad things which are a part of it. If Christ indeed is our life (Colossians 3:4), then:

> ...neither death nor life, neither angels nor demons, neither the present nor the future, nor any powers, neither height nor depth, nor anything else in all creation, will be able to separate us from the love of God that is in Christ Jesus our Lord. (Romans 8:38-39)

Lift up your eyes to heaven and start seeing God as he is and your life through his perspective. Then, and only then, can you be joyful and thankful in all circumstances. And only then will you be obeying the succinct, but weighty, challenges of 1 Thessalonians 5:16-18: "Be joyful always; pray continually; give thanks in all circumstances, for this is God's will for you in Christ Jesus." Focus.

Growing in Gratitude

In what areas of life do you tend to look longingly at the blessings of others and lose your gratitude for what you have? How will you change this?

Do you tend to focus more on the positives or the negatives in your life? In the lives of other people?

Are you willing to ask three close friends to evaluate you regarding the above question? I urge you to do it— you may learn some important things about yourself.

3

Solitary Places

> Very early in the morning, while it was still dark, Jesus got up, left the house and went off to a solitary place, where he prayed.
>
> Mark 1:35

When gratitude causes us to arise early in the morning to spend time with God, we are seeing one of its greatest fruits. Of course, other things will also cause people to pray, and these too are valid. Perhaps it is a prayer of desperation over the illness of a child or another family member. Perhaps it is a prayer of repentance concerning some sin that has left you bleeding spiritually. Perhaps it is a major life decision that has to be made. But arising to pray just because you are thankful to your Maker and Redeemer is the finest reason to seek him out every morning.

Years ago, I remember trying to influence one of my traditional church friends and his wife to really consider the discipling approach to life and ministry. The wife wanted to know in no uncertain terms if they would be *required* to have a quiet time in the morning, or if they could choose any time they wanted. My heart sank. Here was a prideful woman, though religious, already resisting the possibility of anyone being able to advise her to do anything. I tried to use Biblical examples and practical reasons for having morning prayer times, but sadly, in her case, to no avail. Personally, I am grateful for all advice which has improved my walk with God, including that which has helped me establish morning prayer times.

Jesus, the most spiritual person ever to set foot on Earth, was intent on having such times with his Father. David, a man who teaches us so much about seeking and finding God, did the same.

> Give ear to my words, O Lord,
>   consider my sighing.
> Listen to my cry for help,
>   my King and my God,
>   for to you I pray.
> In the morning, O Lord, you hear my voice;
>   in the morning I lay my requests before you
>   and wait in expectation. (Psalm 5:1-3)

In a legalistic sense, no one could say that quiet times must take place in the morning (and I recognize that some people work the second and third shifts and have very different schedules), but these scriptures and practical considerations convince me of the wisdom of such. When I pray and meditate to begin my day, it always goes better than the days when I try to work a time in later in the day. I have found that waiting until later means that I will end up with less time in quantity and quality, and my "connection" with God will not be the same.

Learning to pray is not especially easy, and unless we have someone to really teach us, it can be very difficult. The apostles understood this principle, for they asked Jesus to teach them to pray (Luke 11:1). In my traditional church background as a minister, no one taught me to pray. We prayed at mealtimes and to open and close religious assemblies, but not much prayer occurred otherwise in the lives of those I knew best. I still remember a teacher from a Christian college talking about a little booklet about quiet times, and sharing how he started each day reading the Bible devotionally and praying in a quiet place. To my knowledge, this was the first time I had heard someone speak about quiet times who really had them. I thought it was a novel concept. It was novel enough to me that I remember his presentation a couple of decades later!

I learned to pray when I sensed that I would come apart at the seams emotionally unless I didn't. I was about thirty-eight or thirty-nine, and felt something like a midlife crisis coming on. Years in a traditional ministry had taken its toll, as had my own disconnectedness from God. From my experience, I developed the opinion that such crises occur when we get too tired to hold up the facade any longer, and the real "us" just comes out in plain view!

Thankfully, when I hit this point, God had provided me with a solitary place right under my nose. Our house was on a rather large lot, with room behind it for a seriously large garage. The house was old, but the garage was new—and very spacious (just over one thousand square feet). The church for which I preached had remodeled about two-thirds of it into a heated room for teen classes and activities. It was far enough from the house that I did not feel conspicuous when praying or singing or crying loudly.

I quickly discovered three things that have served my prayer life well. One, I have to be in a solitary place where I don't feel that others may be overhearing my prayers. Two, when I am praying alone, I have to walk and pray. When praying with others, being on my knees with my eyes closed is wonderful, but alone in this position, my mind tends to wander. So, I am a walker. Three, I have to pray aloud. Inner feelings have to be turned into thoughts to be understood, and thoughts have to be condensed to be understandable. Talking forces thoughts through a smaller opening (even if you are a "big mouth"!) and they take shape better.

Furthermore, writing forces feelings through an even smaller opening, and can be one of the best ways to get in touch with feelings when simply praying is not working as well as one would like. In recent months, the value of writing has been extolled by therapists as a way to successfully deal with negative emotions. My wife has been advocating this approach for years, and finally, I have started listening to her! On several occasions last year, I had to take the time to write in depth to figure out what all of my feelings were when facing some serious challenges. Not only was I able to recognize exactly what was going on inside, but also getting it down on paper (or electronically for me) enabled me to have mastery over it and to come up with specific plans to alleviate the problems.

I am very thankful that God has, from that time in my big garage, put me where solitary places were easily available. When we moved from that location, I had some desolate mountaintops near our house in San Diego. I hardly ever saw another person on those little "fire roads," as they were called. I did see foxes, quail and one big snake! But I was able to walk those hills and pour out my heart to God.

I remember the prayer time in January 1986 when my folks were visiting and my dad was sick. We finally went to enough doctors that one diagnosed the real problem. Daddy and I were in that doctor's office when he informed us that Dad had cancer. Those hills were a gift of God the next morning as I prayed and wept to him.

When we moved to Boston, our first place had a great little basement with windows large enough to allow me to see the frequent snowfalls as I walked and prayed. Coming from sunny southern California, that was a special treat. Then in the spring of that year I found a state preserve with multitudes of trails through the woods and around lakes and rivers. Just thinking about it makes me grateful for God's provisions. The next house had not only a good basement, but a wonderful park just down the street, also replete with trails through some beautiful woods.

Following that, we lived next to another preserve for three years. I spent hundreds of early mornings walking and praying there. It was during this time that our nest emptied of children and my father died. Tears come to my eyes as I write this, for I could not have survived those moments without such a solitary place.

The next place we lived did not have any private places close by, so I drove to some woods which were excellent. For many weeks, I first stopped at a coffee shop to share my faith early in the day and to buy coffee and two muffins. I enjoyed them as I read the Bible in the car, and then I walked in those woods and prayed. I can still remember some life-changing prayer times there.

The next place (gee, we've moved a lot) also had nothing close, but the basement was good, and we were there only six months. Then the next place was really great, with a railroad track through the woods and a nearby cemetery as well. Both locations hold some special memories for me with my God. The next two houses had good basements and nearby woods. The one we live in now has some wonderful "town woods" nearby, and a railroad track through another wood.

Solitary places have not been optional or occasional for me, but a daily need. I don't mean to imply that I can get to these places every day, but certainly the more it happens, the better I am.

I have always loved the hymn that speaks of how "God and I go in the fields together," walking and talking "as good friends should and do." It really catches the essence of what these times mean to me. One of my favorite ways to spend a prayer time is just to talk back through all of my solitary places with God and to recount the challenges and the victories he has given me over many years. I never do that without tears of gratitude flowing freely, even as I remember some tears of anguish and how he ultimately gave me and mine the victories. There can be no gratitude without prayer, and there can be no great prayers for guys like me without those solitary places.

"Very early in the morning, while it was still dark, Jesus got up, left the house and went off to a solitary place, where he prayed." (Mark 1:35).

Let's imitate him.

Growing in Gratitude

Do you normally pray out loud during your prayer times? If not, will you try it?

Do you know the type of prayer settings and postures that seem to work best for you, and do you characteristically seek and use them?

How are you feeling right now about the quality of your quiet times, and practically, what can you do to improve them?

4

An Uncommon Peace

Let the peace of Christ rule in your hearts,
since as members of one body you were called
to peace. And be thankful.

Colossians 3:15

hank God for a church characterized by peace.
Some of you reading this book likely have no idea how
little peace exists in most churches. A certain joke that
made the rounds when I was preaching for a different
group of churches illustrates the point well. When asked
what different families in the church were having for
Sunday lunch, the answer came back: fried preacher,
baked elder and stewed deacon! In a figurative way, the
joke was right on target. The last such congregation for
which I preached was one of the worst. As the preacher,
I was the subject of some pretty vicious comments by
certain members. When I weathered the criticism reasonably well, the critics turned their attention to our
children. Suffice it to say that it was not an easy time in
our lives.

After becoming a part of the discipling churches, a young
woman from my former congregation visited the San Diego
church. After services she came up to me somewhat in

shock. She said something to this effect: "Gordon, these people view you like you are Moses or something. Do you think that's a right thing to do?" My answer was quick and sure: "Absolutely! If their high estimate of me and other leaders feeds our pride, then that is our problem, which God will most certainly deal with. But it is quite Biblical to esteem and respect leaders." I went on to tell her that this uncommon appreciation and peace did nothing but humble me and make me extremely grateful to God for allowing me the exalted privilege of leading such a group. You see, we leaders know our own foibles all too well and understand that God's use of us is totally a matter of grace.

Sometimes I talk to an old friend or relative who is still a part of the churches to which I once belonged, and the stories they tell of the lack of peace leave me incredulous. How do people live with such things? How did I ever live with them? The answer is that we did not know it really could be different. Having never seen anything better, we assumed that the status quo was entrenched for the duration. Praise God that peace in the one body of Christ is possible, yea more, is *present*—all over the world. Amen, Hallelujah!

What enables us to have such uncommon peace? Probably the key word is "commonality," for we share so many essential things in common. But three of these items are unquestionably at the very top of the list of essentials. One is our relationship with God and the nature of that relationship. All of us were baptized into Christ only after the decision to truly make Jesus the Lord of our lives. It was not a selfish decision simply to get saved; it was a selfless decision to surrender our lives in representing him to our fellow man. Therefore, we are intent on imitating him and doing what pleases him. He is, and forever must remain, our top priority in life.

A second essential that ensures unity is based on that decision to make Jesus the Lord of our lives. This decision means that everyone will be discipled, which ensures in turn that a lack of peace simply will not be tolerated. If we have a problem with another disciple, we go to them or they come to us for resolution. Actually, we should be going to them *as* they are coming to us, for in Matthew 5:23-24 Jesus says that we should go to the other person if we have offended them, and in Matthew 18:15-16 he says that we should pursue reconciliation if we are the one offended. Hence, we have God's double indemnity spiritual life insurance policy which guarantees the dividend of our uncommon peace.

The third essential is that disciples also have the same basic mission—to seek and save the lost. When we are in the battle together, we are not very likely to attack one another. Persecution from a common enemy as we seek to carry out our mission will actually unify us even more if we view and handle it Biblically. An all-out commitment to the mission and to discipling is what separates us from other religious groups. The first gives us our purpose in life and the second, the only means by which it can be accomplished. My book *Discipling* is subtitled *God's Plan to Train and Transform His People.* If we as a movement, and as individuals within that movement, stay committed to God with the mission and discipling firmly in place, our unity will remain. Obviously, if we begin to waver on either, unity will be threatened.

How can we tell if such wavering is beginning? Since our oneness is the demonstration to the world that we are Christ's (John 17:20-23), this question must be asked and answered. We cannot afford to condone any deviation from the unity for which Jesus prayed—and died. Not surprisingly, our unity will always be inseparably connected with the three basics mentioned above.

Biblically, the "daily diet" of the healthy disciple consists of these basics. We are to spend time in the Word daily (Acts 17:11) and in prayer (Luke 11:1-4), both of which are elements in our relationship with God. We are to share our faith daily (Acts 17:17) and be open with our lives daily with one another (Hebrews 3:12). Therefore, the first warning sign of approaching disunity comes when we as individuals do not have our relationship with God as our top priority. When either the quantity or quality of time with him is compromised, sin will enter and ultimately permeate the whole of our spiritual lives. Are you having consistent times with God? Are you emotionally connecting with him during those times? Spirituality comes from this relationship, and without spirituality there cannot be unity.

A second warning sign appears when there is a lack of commitment to and involvement in the mission of evangelism. Paul's little letter to Philemon contains this remarkable statement:

> I pray that you may be active in sharing your faith,
> so that you will have a full understanding of every
> good thing we have in Christ. (Philemon 1:6)

While the context of this verse is likely referring most directly to the sharing of faith and lives with other Christians (Paul uses here the word *koinonia* which is the word for "fellowship" in Acts 2:42), all sharing of our faith builds our faith. Appreciation for our life in Christ grows with our sharing of it. Evangelism is not just to save the souls of the lost; it is designed to keep the souls of the saved, saved.

When we are studying the Bible with others, thus going back through why we became disciples in the first place, our hearts and convictions are strengthened incredibly. We remain excited and thankful about the amazing life that God has given us in Christ. Therefore, if evangelism has become humdrum to us, a burden and not a blessing, a duty and not a desire, we are slipping into the sins described in Revelation 2 and 3: loss of our first love and lukewarmness. If you are not in the mission heart and soul right now, Satan is into his mission with you, heart and soul. Wake up and repent!

A third warning sign is actually much more subtle and deceptive than the other two. It of course ties in to the discipling process. Are we being discipled? Do we *want* to be discipled? Are we consistently seeking lots of advice—and following it? Are we being open with what is in our heart of hearts? Do we *want* to be open—with everything? The honest answers to those questions will go a long way in helping you evaluate where you are right now in your relationships with other people. Satan is a master at encouraging us to be open only up to a point, not sharing the most difficult things to share—which will always be the most important ones! We may have quiet reservations about the church or other people, and we keep them inside, rationalizing that we cannot possibly confess everything anyway. Obviously, while we cannot literally confess every detail about every subject, we must have a deep conviction about exposing our reservations and living daily with a spirit of openness.

The depth of unity for which Jesus prayed cannot be overstated. Read the following verses very carefully and ask yourself how well you are fulfilling them:

All the believers were one in heart and mind. No one claimed that any of his possessions was his own, but they shared everything they had. (Acts 4:32)

Let us therefore make every effort to do what leads to peace and to mutual edification. (Romans 14:19)

May the God who gives endurance and encouragement give you a spirit of unity among yourselves as you follow Christ Jesus, so that with one heart and mouth you may glorify the God and Father of our Lord Jesus Christ. (Romans 15:5-6)

I appeal to you, brothers, in the name of our Lord Jesus Christ, that all of you agree with one another so that there may be no divisions among you and that you may be perfectly united in mind and thought. (1 Corinthians 1:10)

Finally, brothers, good-by. Aim for perfection, listen to my appeal, be of one mind, live in peace. And the God of love and peace will be with you. (2 Corinthians 13:11)

Make every effort to keep the unity of the Spirit through the bond of peace. (Ephesians 4:3)

Whatever happens, conduct yourselves in a manner worthy of the gospel of Christ. Then, whether I come and see you or only hear about you in my absence, I will know that you stand firm in one spirit, contending as one man for the faith of the gospel. (Philippians 1:27)

> Then make my joy complete by being like-minded, having the same love, being one in spirit and purpose. (Philippians 2:2)

> Finally, all of you, live in harmony with one another; be sympathetic, love as brothers, be compassionate and humble. (1 Peter 3:8)

The inclusion of these verses and many more like them in sacred Scripture is proof positive that oneness in God's kingdom is more important than we can begin to imagine. As our movement grows and leaders associate mainly with those within their world sectors, the maintenance of Biblical oneness will present a growing challenge. But nothing is quite as precious as the unity we now enjoy. Make sure that you are always a part of the solution and never a part of the problem in this vital area. As the Psalmist said in the long ago, "How good and pleasant it is when brothers live together in unity!" (Psalm 133:1). Realize what a precious commodity our peace is, be grateful for it, and fight Satan with all that you have in order to maintain it.

Growing in Gratitude

How well are you currently doing in each of the daily basics of Christianity: prayer, time in the Word, evangelism and being open with others about your life?

What unspiritual attitudes and hidden sins have you not confessed? When will you?

Toward whom do you have unresolved issues that you need to talk through with them? Write down your plan to do so, and follow through with it.

5

Free at Last, Free at Last!

What a wretched man I am! Who will rescue me from this body of death? Thanks be to God— through Jesus Christ our Lord!

Romans 7:24-25

*O*n August 28, 1963, Martin Luther King delivered a keynote speech in Washington, D.C., to an audience of more than 200,000 civil rights supporters that is normally called his "I Have a Dream" speech. He expressed the hopes of the civil rights movement, and among many stirring statements was this one:

I have a dream that my four little children will one day live in a nation where they will not be judged by the color of their skin but by the content of their character.

When King went on to shout, "Free at last, free at last," he was speaking to the hearts of millions who longed to enjoy freedom from all types of oppression.

Slavery in America ended when the Emancipation Proclamation issued by President Lincoln on January 1, 1863, became reality with the thirteenth amendment to the Constitution, passed by Congress in January and ratified by the states in December 1865. The period of slavery in America was the nation's ugliest chapter, and the effects of it have been difficult to overcome. What became official in 1865 did not end the practical problems, nor has the passage of more than a century. Time just doesn't heal all wounds. The more subtle effects of slavery can exist long after freedoms are granted by legislation. As we will see, this principle applies in another arena as well.

As bad as slavery in America was, another type of slavery is even worse—the slavery of sin. Its impact goes far beyond this life, reaching into eternity. Paul described this dreadful malady in these words:

> Don't you know that when you offer yourselves to someone to obey him as slaves, you are slaves to the one whom you obey—whether you are slaves to sin, which leads to death, or to obedience, which leads to righteousness? (Romans 6:16)

Unquestionably, sin enslaves, destroys and damns. For this reason, God sent his Son into the world, and "God made him who had no sin to be sin for us, so that in him we might become the righteousness of God" (2 Corinthians 5:21). However, the existence and availability of righteousness does not ensure that we will receive it, even if we seek it. Our understanding of how to accept it can be amiss, for Satan has worked overtime to fill the world with false teachings in the realm of Christianity. One of his favorite tools to divert us from the genuine article is legalistic religion. When Paul penned the words of Romans 7, he was addressing this problem.

The Jews of the first century were very committed to their religion. They had seen what disobedience to the Law had done historically to their ancestors—how they had been beaten down by foreign powers and delivered into decades of captivity. The following generations were determined not to follow in those same paths. So, they had built a "wall" of sorts around the Law to make sure that they did not get close to violating it. General commands were studied meticulously and rules were made to protect the people from the possibility of disobeying the commands. The end result of this approach was a religion mired down by regulations. The means to the desired end, righteousness by grace, led to a different entity entirely: legalistic righteousness by works. Men judged other men not on the content of their character, but on the basis of their conformity to the rules. In a nutshell, they majored in the minors and minored in the majors.

In the book of Romans, Paul, as a trained rabbinic scholar, systematically reasoned through the process of grace through faith as the only way to salvation. After showing that the world was totally condemned by sin (Romans 1-3), he held up Abraham as one who was justified by grace rather than by works (Romans 4). He proceeded to show the essentiality of Christ's death for man's righteousness (Romans 5), followed by a description of how men can die to sin and to legalism (Romans 6-7). The high-water mark of Romans comes in chapter eight, the message of which could aptly be called, "Free at last, free at last." However, he could not quite wait until Romans 8 to shout those words. As he was finishing his argument in Romans 7 about the huge weight of legalistic religion, he wrote:

> What a wretched man I am! Who will rescue me from this body of death? Thanks be to God—through Jesus Christ our Lord! (Romans 7:24-25)

To understand his exuberance, we need to read the preceding verses in Romans 7:

> For in my inner being I delight in God's law; but I see another law at work in the members of my body, waging war against the law of my mind and making me a prisoner of the law of sin at work within my members. What a wretched man I am! Who will rescue me from this body of death? (Romans 7:22-24)

Paul was trying to make those with legalistic mind-sets admit to themselves the turmoil going on inside their hearts and consciences. (A good title for a sermon from this passage would be, "Will Somebody Please Help the Two of Me!") A religion based on performance is doomed to yield these kinds of results. The more we focus on ourselves and what we *must* do to please God, the more we end up in frustration and failure. The answer to this dilemma is to focus on God and what he has already done for us, and then we end up serving him out of heartfelt gratitude. No greater example of this principle could be given than the example of the very one who penned these words, Paul. He said this of himself in 1 Corinthians 15:10:

> But by the grace of God I am what I am, and his grace to me was not without effect. No, I worked harder than all of them—yet not I, but the grace of God that was with me.

I have many memories of being raised in a legalistic religion. We condemned others outwardly and ourselves inwardly. We too discussed the minutia of the law and argued vehemently against those who differed with us doctrinally. We had little room for the exercise of individual opinions and for that reason never spent much time studying Romans 14 (which is all about such differences). Everything became a matter of right and wrong, rarely good, better and best; to err on one point might well put our souls in eternal jeopardy. Our hearts were always focused on whether we had done enough and had done it right. Having security in our salvation was an illusory concept at best. After all, we could have prayed one more prayer, given one more dollar, taught one more person and read one more chapter. "Have we done enough?" was the question that haunted our souls. No wonder Paul could not wait to shout out, "Who will rescue me from this body of death? Thanks be to God—through Jesus Christ our Lord!"

In years gone by I have known people who have left the church and who later said they were much happier after they left. For a long time I strongly doubted their statement about being happier, assuming that deep inside, their consciences must be condemning them. However, I came to realize that most of those who leave God's church and express such opinions about what they now feel have a very skewed view of Christianity. They may have been performance based, and any escape from the misery of a Romans 7 mentality is a welcome relief (regardless of where it puts them with God).

People who have escaped Romans 7 in the right way, by adopting the glorious promises of Romans 8, would never leave God and his church. Their focus is not on themselves, but on him who died for them. They do not work to be saved, but *because* they are saved. They delight in the law of God, to be sure, but for many reasons—one of which is that as the mirror of their souls (James 1:23-25), the law points out their sin clearly, making them feel even more indebted to the God who continually and graciously forgives all of their sins.

Read Romans 7:14-25 carefully. Do you often feel this inner turmoil in your heart? If so, you are walking the tightrope of a legalistic approach to God, which will likely result in you giving up at some point. The only motivation for serving God which can last a lifetime is our love responding to his grace. Fear may get our attention (and that is valid), but it will not keep it to the same degree. Christian fellowship may attract us at first (also a valid factor—John 13:34-35), but it will not keep us faithful forever. Ambition may motivate us for a while, but it cannot sustain us when disappointments and failures take their toll. When we really understand God's unconditional love for us, our hearts are set free to serve in a way that most religious people never fathom. It is the difference between religion that is *desire* and not simply *duty*; religion that is *delight* and not *drudgery*; religion that is *heart-deep* and not simply *habit-deep!* God does not say, "Measure up and I'll accept you," for no one ever measures up. Rather, he says, "I'll accept you in Christ, and now you and I will walk and work together in my strength."

"Thanks be to God for his indescribable gift!" (2 Corinthians 9:15). By his grace and goodness, we can shout from the mountaintops, "Free at last, free at last! Praise God!"

Growing in Gratitude

In what areas do you struggle with legalism? Find and memorize a scripture to help you change in each of these areas.

When do you most often feel like you are living in Romans 7 rather than Romans 8? List some examples.

Are you normally more focused on God or on your necessary response to him? How will you change?

6

Thank God I'm a Country Boy!

> But who are you, O man, to talk back to God?
> "Shall what is formed say to him who formed it,
> 'Why did you make me like this?'" Does not the
> potter have the right to make out of the same
> lump of clay some pottery for noble purposes
> and some for common use?
>
> Romans 9:20-21

I am not what you would call a country music buff. I do have a few CDs in that category, and when a certain mood strikes me, I may pull out one and listen to Garth Brooks sing about his "friends in low places." Much of that stuff is pretty comical to me. A couple of years back, when we went to see our son, Bryan, he couldn't wait to tell me about a country-and-western song he had recently heard. He said, "It's you, Dad!" I took the bait and asked what it was, to which he replied, "High Tech Redneck." Well, I can't deny being a country boy from Louisiana, which in the estimate of most people is not one of our more impressive states. And my family actually had red necks from doing construction work in that hot sun. Being into computers and little electronic gizmos does qualify me as somewhat high tech, so I couldn't argue that the song applied to me.

The issue is that whatever our background may be, we cannot change it. We must trust God with it and do whatever we can within our context to make ourselves useful to him (see 2 Timothy 2:20-21). When it comes to our background, we are who we are. Parts of our lives that are out of our hands we must learn to accept.

Now all of this is far easier said than done. All of us have things about ourselves that we wish were different. Maybe it is our nose or our teeth or our hair or our brain or our height or our body build or any one of dozens of attributes. Maybe it is our cultural heritage or our race or our education or our parents. Some of these things we can change to some degree, but many of them we cannot. We must simply accept them—even be grateful for them—and then use them to God's glory.

I am a country boy with a redneck background, which has not always been easy for me to accept. Steve Johnson's descriptions of himself in his book, *I Wanna Hear Him Say, 'Well Done,'* do make it easier for me, I must say. But this is actually a serious chapter about accepting, with grace, who God made you. He is the Potter and we are but clay.

I remember a few years back when I was trying to figure out what kind of people intimidated me in evangelism and why. The more I thought and prayed about it, the clearer it became: American, white, professional men. But why? That's simple. My blue-collar relatives tended to be intimidated by this type of person. Actually, we had friends in this category, but in general we felt inferior to the more educated, more successful people. In thinking about it, I realized that I was not intimidated by those from other races, nor even by whites from other countries. I was raised believing that Americans of any type were superior to any other nationality. (Yes, I know this is wrong, bigoted, and stupid—I'm just talking about my roots for a minute.)

Of course, through the years, in terms of education and lifestyle, I became the very kind of person who intimidated me. But the roots go deep until we dig them out. Just when I could have started feeling less conspicuous in my cultural heritage, what did God do? He moved me to Boston! Hardly a single day goes by that people, upon hearing my Southern accent, don't ask, "Where in the world are you from?" Now they may not utter all of those exact words verbally, but it is often in their tone. Frankly, I get tired of hearing it. Why couldn't God work it out for me to have been raised in the Midwest or let me stay in the South? Oh yes, I remember—I'm just the clay.

During that particular time of introspection, I tried to figure out the main things that I didn't like about myself, that I had allowed to become a part of this intimidation business. One was the accent. Another was my blue-collar roots. And a third is my nonathletic body build, which corresponds perfectly to my athletic ability, by the way. I could add other things under the physical appearance category, like my schnoz, but I ended up with these three basic categories on my list. One morning during a prayer walk in the woods, a thought hit me like a bolt out of the blue. I thought about those passages in Hebrews which say that Jesus was tempted in all points, just as we are, and could therefore sympathize with us (Hebrews 2:18; 4:15-16). Then I began looking at his life in terms of the three categories on my list.

What about his cultural heritage? He was from Galilee (bad) and Nazareth (worse). He was a carpenter's son and then a carpenter himself—an uneducated, blue-collar man, wouldn't you say, at least from the world's viewpoint? But how about the physical appearance part? Isaiah makes it clear that Jesus would not have won any "most handsome" contests in Nazareth or any other place: "He had no beauty or majesty to attract us to him, nothing in his appearance that we should desire him" (Isaiah 53:2). I was feeling much better already! Now, what about the one which presents my biggest challenge—the accent? God covered that one pretty well also.

When the apostles stood up to speak on Pentecost in the environs of the Harvard of Judaism, what did people notice first? "Utterly amazed, they asked: 'Are not all these men who are speaking Galileans?'" (Acts 2:7). In context, they wondered how these men could be speaking in all of the other languages. They could have wondered that about anyone who chanced to speak that day, but they really wondered about it in the case of Galileans. The capital city of Judaism in every way was Jerusalem in Judea. Anybody who *was* anybody was either from there or had at least been trained there (like Paul). Otherwise, you were not really educated. If you were from a place like Galilee, you were, in the eyes of the elite of Judaism, well, a hick, a country boy, a redneck.

Why did God have his son born in Galilee and all the original disciples chosen from there? Paul himself addressed that one in 1 Corinthians 1:26-29:

> Brothers, think of what you were when you were called. Not many of you were wise by human standards; not many were influential; not many were of noble birth. But God chose the foolish things of the world to shame the wise; God chose the weak things of the world to shame the strong. He chose the lowly things of this world and the despised things—

and the things that are not—to nullify the things that are, so that no one may boast before him. (1 Corinthians 1:26-29)

God loves this stuff, going against the grain of the worldly, and he wants us to learn to laugh at ourselves a bit. He made us all kind of funny in different ways, to persuade us that the power is in him, not in us. And regarding the lost, he is trying to show them something as well, in using the likes of us to do his bidding. Whatever it is about you that you have difficulty accepting, loosen up. Take a good look at those first ragtag disciples, and a good physical look at the One who led them. God moves in mysterious ways, his wonders to perform, and we need to decide that whatever he did to make us who we are has a purpose in the whole scheme of things.

Jesus understands and he sympathizes with what we feel. He faced the same temptations we do and never gave up or gave in. We sometimes think that his failure to sin makes it harder for him to really understand us, but we are missing something when we think this way. We endure only a certain amount of temptation usually, and then give in, which means that we do not understand full-strength temptation. Jesus understands the full strength of *every* temptation precisely *because* he never gave in to it. No one knows more about temptations than he. Trust him. He so identified himself with mankind that somehow his life on earth provides us with the help we need to face the challenges that come. Whatever you have trouble accepting about yourself, chances are you can discover something similar that he handled with both grace and gratitude.

"Thank God I'm a country boy," goes the song. Let's get happy with who he made us, and then use it all for his glory. He has a plan for you, and he does not make mistakes in bringing it to fruition. Thank God for Jesus!

> For we do not have a high priest who is unable to sympathize with our weaknesses, but we have one who has been tempted in every way, just as we are— yet was without sin. Let us then approach the throne of grace with confidence, so that we may receive mercy and find grace to help us in our time of need. (Hebrews 4:15-16)

Growing in Gratitude

Make a list of the "unchangeables" about yourself that you do not like.

Think of ways that Jesus could identify with you in facing these things about yourself.

Share these things with at least two other people and determine to surrender them to God, accept who you are, and let God use (unique) you!

Bon Appetit!

For everything God created is good, and nothing is to be rejected if it is received with thanksgiving.

1 Timothy 4:4

*I*t was one of those relaxed mornings to just bask in the thought, "Life is good." Theresa and I had arrived in Madrid, Spain, the night before and had enjoyed a full night's sleep (for a welcome change). I then sat in a restaurant housed within a magnificent European train station, awaiting the arrival of my young friend, Jose (not his real name). He had sent word through Juan, the leader of the church in Madrid, that he really needed to see me. According to Juan, Jose had been struggling spiritually for some time. I knew the young man well enough to know that he had what I call an accused personality.

Revelation 12:9-10 tells us that Satan works to both deceive us and accuse us. People tend either toward having a deceived conscience or an accused one. If the former, they don't have much awareness of their sins, and if the latter, they are far too aware of them and often struggle with being "down on themselves." Many (most?) spiritually minded people seem to be of the accused variety, although I know some outstanding male ministry leaders who are definitely in the deceived category. Thankfully, their wives are more aware of their mate's sins and are able to help these deceived brothers who seldom struggle with guilt feelings to understand the rest of the population. By their own admission, these brothers married a conscience (thank God!).

But back to the story in Madrid. As I was waiting for Juan and Jose to arrive for our lunch appointment, I couldn't help but marvel at the surroundings. The main part of the train station was one large open space with a very high roof and a tropical garden of sorts on the ground floor, complete with dense foliage and palm trees. The restaurant was on a second level without many exterior walls, allowing a fairly unobstructed view of the rest of the station below. The restaurant was a nice one and started to be filled mostly by rather highpowered business types. For nearly half an hour, I just enjoyed peering through the almost ethereal haze caused by the moisture generated by the foliage and its irrigation system.

After the two young brothers arrived for lunch and we had exchanged greetings and ordered our food, I decided not to move quickly into the discussion about Jose's spiritual condition. The more uncomfortable he seemed to be with the delay, the more relaxed and jovial I became. He seemed to have trouble computing my mood, apparently thinking something along these lines, *Doesn't Gordon know that I'm not doing well spiritually?* But I surmised that his condition was a lot darker and uglier in his mind than in God's. This is nearly always true in persons with an accused personality. So I kept enjoying the wonderful ambiance and stayed lighthearted in spite of his melancholy mood. God was still on his throne, and life was good!

After about fifteen more minutes, I finally broached the subject and asked Jose how he was doing. "Not so good," he said. "I've been struggling for quite a while in my relationship with God." I asked if he wanted to do well with God. "Of course," he said, with a look that showed his surprise that I would even ask the question.

Then I asked another question: "Are you really sorry about the time of not doing well in your relationship with God?" Again, the quick answer was definitely affirmative. Then, a third question: "If we can come up with a good plan of repentance, are you willing to follow it?"

"Absolutely," came his answer.

"Great," I said. "Bon appetit!"

At this point, poor Jose was quite in shock. *Where was the rebuke?* he seemed to wonder. But in my mind, he did a much better job of beating on himself than I could do, and I was certain that his view of God's fatherhood was quite different from mine. Being the father of two grown children, I know what loving fathers want for their children: they want them to be happy. When the kids aren't doing well, I just want them to repent as quickly as possible and then get happy again. If this is my strong desire for my children, just think how much more God desires this for his children!

Too many of us seem to think that God turns away from us when we are doing badly and turns back to us when we repent. Actually, fathers are much more engaged when their kids are not doing well. Our phone bills go up when our kids are facing challenges, but otherwise the calls are more occasional. I think that the Bible clearly indicates that God turns to us most when we need help the most. Obviously, if we are intent on following the route of the lost son in Luke 15, only learning lessons the hard way, God will allow us to leave his care. But for those of us wanting and trying to live as disciples, our problem times attract his attention and help like a magnet attracts metal. Even a cursory reading of such passages as John 3:16-17 and Romans 5:6-11 will demonstrate the point clearly. If God *ran* to hug the returning prodigal son in Luke 15, with the stench of the pig pen in his clothes, you can be sure that he will do everything possible to help those of us who are struggling but trying.

I began explaining some of these principles to Jose in order to persuade him to accept the time of refreshing which follows repentance, but somehow he had difficulty believing that it could be this simple. He was like many religious people who confuse "penance" with repentance. We would be much more comfortable trying to work off the sins somehow (which, of course, can never be done). Ten "Hail Marys" and ten "Our Fathers" may satisfy misguided consciences, but they will never satisfy God. Repentance is a change of mind, which, if genuine, results in changed behavior. At the point the mind changes, the conscience should be cleared.

I remember a prayer time back about five years ago on a Monday morning. The week prior had not been a good one for me spiritually. I had not met my own expectations in my daily walk as a disciple in several areas. I recall exactly where I was during that prayer walk when I expressed this sentiment to God: "Lord, I am really sorry about the lukewarm week I had last week, and I promise this week to really work hard and make up for last week." As soon as those words had slipped past my lips, I thought to myself, *Ferguson, that statement reflects some bad theology.*

We cannot offset any sin by any amount of good deeds. Works have their place, but they were never designed to do the undoable: What we have done, our deeds cannot undo. All that we can do is repent, accept the forgiveness gained by Christ's deeds, and then start over again, motivated by God's grace. God is the God of the new beginning, not simply at our rebirth, but every day—or many times a day, if we will but accept his grace. Now that *is* good news!

As I watched Jose's face, I could tell that he was finally starting to understand what I was trying to explain. I looked around once more at the beautiful surroundings and pointed them out to him. "Just look at those trees and plants, Jose. Who do you think God created those for—us or the pagans?"

Back came the incredulous look on his face. *Now what is Gordon talking about?* he seemed to be wondering. I quoted 1 Timothy 4:3, which says that what God created was "to be received with thanksgiving by those who believe and who know the truth." The world may enjoy them, but they are especially made for us who understand enough to give God the praise for them. No one should be in a better position to enjoy the things of this life than the Christian. We know who made them and why!

"This salmon is delightful, Jose. And I think that God made it just for you and me to enjoy today. Isn't that great?"

Not every spiritual problem can be resolved easily, but I believe there is a perspective here that is needed in dealing with any problem. Before that leisurely European lunch was over, some burdens had been lifted and some lines on foreheads relaxed. Life is pretty short to go through it burdened. This is no fun, and neither is it pleasing to our Father, nor beneficial to us. Sin is serious, to be sure, but this is what the cross was all about. Man owed a debt he could not pay, and Jesus paid a debt he did not owe. Accept that, repent when you need to repent, and make sure your rejoicing times are much, much longer than your burdened times. Feel the burden of sin long enough to be convicted and moved to repentance, but then get on with the refreshing times. Without a doubt this is what God wants for us. Bon appetit! Pass the *crème brulée!*

Growing in Gratitude

Is your conscience more of the accused variety or the deceived type? If you're not sure, ask a spiritual friend who knows you well.

After committing which sins do you feel the most burdened? How long do you usually carry that burden? How has this chapter helped you?

What are the dangers of taking sin too seriously? Too lightly?

8

Don't Waste Your Sin!

> But Joseph said to them, "Don't be afraid. Am I
> in the place of God? You intended to harm me,
> but God intended it for good to accomplish what
> is now being done, the saving of many lives."
>
> Genesis 50:19-20

I remember hearing a brother tell the story of his pre-Christian life, and without doubt his past was sordid. There was little in the Biblical catalog of sins that he had not done. At the end of it all, I was almost speechless in the pity I felt for him. I needed to respond and reassure him, but the right words were slow in coming. Finally, I simply said, "Don't waste your sin." By that I meant that he could use his past to encourage others that they could also overcome their sin, for almost anyone could identify with something from his life. Did not Paul do the same thing when he called himself the chief of sinners? (1 Timothy 1:15-16). He was saying that if God could save him, then God could save anyone. Paul was not wasting his sin, but using it as an example of the magnitude of God's grace.

Whether it is our own sin or the sin others have committed against us, sin should not be wasted. In God's

incredible plan, his grace can take what was initially hurtful and turn it for good. The story of Joseph in the Old
Testament shows that he was not blind to the value of his
brothers' sins against him. With his spiritual grasp of life,
he saw God in it all. When Joseph first revealed himself
to his brothers in Egypt, he told them not to be distressed
or angry with themselves for selling him into slavery. He
was certain that God had done it all for the purpose of
saving the lives of his family (Genesis 45:5). From this
point until their father Jacob's death, Joseph treated his
brothers very well. But when Jacob died, their smitten
consciences caused them to think that Joseph would turn
against them and get even with them for their horrible
sins against him in his youth. They approached him with
the story that Jacob had directed them to come and ask
for forgiveness once more.

Whether Jacob actually gave the direction is uncertain
in my mind. Perhaps he did, but if so, it was only because
he knew the state of their guilty consciences, not because
he questioned Joseph's heart toward them. Upon hearing
their plea, Joseph wept (Genesis 50:17) and assured them
that God had used their sin for a greater good. Obviously,
Joseph was correct in his assessment of the situation, and
in being correct, he saved himself a lifetime of bitterness
and self-pity.

Until and unless we see God's presence in our challenges, we are going to sin and sin greatly. When something

in our lives seems very unfair and perhaps overwhelming in its effects, we had better start looking for the hand of God in it all. Somehow, some way, some day it will all make sense. No matter what happens, God intends to use it for good.

One of the best illustrations of the above principle I have ever personally seen was in the life of an evangelist in the Paris church, a brother named Alex. With his permission, I would like to share his story and the difference it has made in him when he learned the lesson that Joseph learned centuries ago.

I asked to talk with Alex originally because he seemed to be passively resistant and rebellious, and very locked up emotionally. His wife of four years had never seen him cry until that day, and she rightly assumed that much of his emotional state traced back to his being an adopted child. As he began to tell his story, it was easy to understand some of the negative effects in his life that we were seeing. He was born in Africa, a child of a racially mixed relationship: his father was white French and his mother was black African; they were unmarried. When he was born, his eighteen-year-old mother gave him up immediately to her mother, and for the first several years of his life, Alex was raised by his grandmother. However, in their Muslim environment, half-white kids were roundly rejected. So, he had early memories of being different and feeling rejected by other children, but perhaps mostly by adults. At about age four, he was placed in an orphanage, for reasons unknown to him.

Alex's future adoptive parents were working in Africa and knew his biological father and of Alex's existence. They started taking him home with them for the weekends and after a year and a half, adopted him. His mother and grandmother were evidently at the orphanage for the adoption signing, but he has no memory of this. His adoptive parents moved back to France, which meant that he had to cope with being raised in a white man's world as a racially mixed child. Combine this with the inability of his parents to express love in a way meaningful to him, and he was set up to do lots of rebelling, which he did. He had many fights with those who ridiculed him, a sad situation for a little boy to continually face. He developed patterns of rebellion and failure, which ended up pervading his character.

The second time we got together, I assigned him the task of writing out anything emotional he could remember from his past, which led to the discovery of his feelings of rejection and failure. For the third (and final) session, I asked him to write out his feelings about three areas in his life: rejection (being given up for adoption and being different racially from his adoptive parents); failure; and rebellion.

As Alex wrote, he came up with several good insights, the key being that the three areas were very connected: rejection led to rebellion, which in turn led to failure. However, in the past he did not understand his motivation very well. He discovered that he always tried to prove wrong those who did not believe in him, but was lazy when people did believe in him. I helped him see that rebellion was the root in both cases, for he was refusing to measure up to people's expectations of him—whether good or bad. And, as he built his pattern of rebelling against positive expectations, this forged a weakness in his character: laziness.

Lately, Alex had been feeling flat and unmotivated in ministry—and in life in general. Although he came into the kingdom and into leadership out of some godly motivations, he also had motivations of proving himself. Through his writing time, he realized that after he had achieved most of his main goals as a leader, he then lacked motivation.

Having childhood experiences like Alex's requires finding God's perspective on the situation. No matter what else may be said about why Alex went through what he did, he ended up better off physically (with his adopted parents in France), and, most importantly, he ended up in the kingdom of God. Now, like Joseph, he is to save his people, and guess which two types of people are in his current ministry? African and French!

Additionally, as he was attempting to understand God's hand in his life, he had a great insight about his trip to Sweden where he met the church. He went alone, after having a fight with his friend with whom he was supposed to travel. As a result, he was open to the invitation to attend church, but had his friend been with him, this most likely would not have been the case.

Another key in adjusting to life's difficulties is to put the best possible interpretation on the circumstances. In the case of Alex, the questions of why his mother and grandmother gave him up are important considerations, but he must assume the best scenario, not the worst. His birth mother was young and pregnant by a man who did not want to marry her. She was going to give birth to a mixed-race child, a real challenge in her Muslim society. Perhaps she gave him to her mother to raise simply because she was not able to handle the situation emotionally or even financially. The grandmother faced similar challenges with the prejudice of her friends and the financial burdens in a poor society. Placing him in an orphanage was her best chance at having his physical needs met.

Alex's adoptive parents were, and are, intent on having a loving relationship with Alex and his family. Sure, they had some inadequacies in expressing their love, but is that not common? But look at what they did—they too had to make their explanations about the racial difference (which was a big issue in white France at that time).

We must become thankful rather than resentful or hurt, which means that we must give the benefit of the doubt, assuming the best about the intentions of others. Just look at all that Joseph was thankful for in his situation. Look at all that Alex has to be thankful for in his: He is an evangelist in the kingdom of God, married to a great woman, the father of a beautiful little daughter and is surrounded by kingdom friends.

The most important key to his acceptance of his life and making the needed changes is developing deep gratitude for what God has done through his life's challenges. He must come to peace with his past, but then move on to build a better character by refusing to rebel and by asserting himself to overcome his laziness. But the motivation for both of these actions must be gratitude. I am happy to say that Alex has made much progress. Whereas he used to be late to meetings almost every time, he is now early almost every time. When he is commended and feels the rebellion forming inside, he recognizes it and moves to cut it off. I am really proud of him and look forward to his now becoming all that God designed him to be.

The apostle Paul too had a past to overcome, and grace was his key—which boils down to gratitude. The early apostles were motivated by selfish ambition up to

the time of the cross, but then it seemed to almost entirely dissipate in light of Jesus' death.

Don't waste your own sin, and don't view the sins
of others against you in a humanistic manner. The purposes of God are somehow intertwined with all that has
happened and will happen to you. Develop his perspective on the matters at hand, be gracious in your
evaluation of others' roles in them, and then decide to
be filled with gratitude. God has a plan to use it all for
the saving of souls—yours and many others'. Be a Joseph. Trust God. Forgive yourself and others. And by all
means, use your experiences to encourage others and
to give them hope that if *you* have overcome by God's
grace, so can they. Never waste the impact that your
past can have on others.

Above all, be thankful. Be fully assured that God intends your past to accomplish good, the saving of many
lives for eternity!

Growing in Gratitude

Do you often question God and what he causes or allows to happen in your life?

Which circumstances in you life, perhaps especially others' sins against you, do you have the most trouble accepting?

Have you ever put the effort into seeing God's purpose in each of these instances in order to gain a pure spiritual perspective on them? If not, will you now?

9

Making Peace with the Past

Brothers, I do not consider myself yet to have taken
hold of it. But one thing I do: Forgetting what is
behind and straining toward what is ahead, I press
on toward the goal to win the prize for which God
has called me heavenward in Christ Jesus.

Philippians 3:13-14

*P*utting the past behind us is very important to main-
taining the attitude of gratitude. Obviously, the mistakes
and failures of the past can be debilitating and burden-
some if we spend much time thinking about them. Better
to learn from them, repent of them, and then forget them.
God is the God of new beginnings, but we must let him
be that for us. We also need to put our past successes
behind us (and this may very well be what Paul first had
in mind in this passage). The pop song "Glory Days" is
very sad, as the people in it are thinking back to high
school times when they were more popular and more
athletically skilled. Even in the kingdom, if our glory days
are in the past, we will be ungrateful in the present—and
ineffective in it as well.

For many of us, we can deal with the past and move
on fairly easily. Others of us are going to have to spend

more time dealing with the past because of its present impact on us. A good friend of mine once shared an illustration with me that has proved very useful in helping others make peace with their pasts. This brother had served two stints in Vietnam as a Green Beret commander and knew a lot about the need to work through soul-scarring episodes of life. When he shared with me that about as many Vietnam veterans have died at their own hands since the war as died *in* the war, I realized the importance of learning to help people put the past to rest, God's way.

His illustration was this: Imagine your life as a photo album and start from the back, which represents the present. Thumb back through the pages to the different times in your life. With most of the pages, you will feel settled out, no matter how foolish you may have been at any given point (as in, "Look at that hair!"). When you come to a page that grabs you emotionally, you have unfinished business there. Maybe it was the death of a loved one or some other traumatic event, or a failure of some sort, or any one of a number of things. If you are not settled out emotionally on that time of your life, you need to work through it and lay it to rest. The illustration is very good, because it allows you to follow a very wise adage: If it ain't broke, don't fix it. On the other hand, if it is broken, then it needs to be fixed.

Most of the things that scarred us emotionally in the past are related to family situations in our early years. If we had relatively stable family situations, even though we may have committed many damaging sins in our teen years, we are not likely to have to work through things in our past. In fact, those with such backgrounds often cannot figure out why others would need help working through earlier experiences, since their own pasts contain some pretty bad memories as well. But the issue is normally not what you did to yourself by your own sins, but what others did *to* you, especially in your earliest years.

We cannot become spiritual psychologists in our discipling of one another, but years and years of experience as a people helper have totally convinced me that unless and until some people receive help in dealing with their pasts, they will feel like damaged goods and reap the harvest of such feelings. The real failure of modern psychology is that problems are diagnosed by their origins, but real cures are not applied. Only God has the cure, and he expressed it in the principles of the Bible. Most of the cure, once we have faced our pasts, is found in getting God's perspective and then figuring out how he wants to use these things for good which appear so bad from a human perspective.

My wife has helped many women, especially those who were abused emotionally or sexually, deal with damaging pasts. Her approach is to have the woman write out what happened in some detail and get in touch with the feelings that accompanied the hurtful events. Next the woman needs to figure out how she responded sinfully to the situation(s), which makes it easier to forgive those responsible for the hurt. Then she must decide to give it up to God. She often has sisters simply burn their written accounts once they reach the point of deciding to put it all behind them. It does not have to be a long process, but it is a very important one for those whose pasts continue to plague their hearts in spite of their previous attempts to move past them.

In the chapter prior to this, I related how I had followed this procedure with my friend Alex. Some may be very concerned (overly so, in my opinion) that delving into someone's past will cause us to become Freudian counselors. That is decidedly not the point. Most people do not need such help, but those who do, deserve to receive it. With Alex, we spent three times together for the express purpose of working through his past. He was able to put the past to rest and has definitely moved on. I have no intention of revisiting the events of his past. He received the help he needed and has moved far beyond where he was before. The focus is not at all to cause someone to *live* in the past; it is just the opposite. However, if the past is messing up the present, we had better help the person to deal with it.

Why do you think David wrote so many psalms of such varied natures? I suspect that he had found a way to deal with his own heart emotionally and spiritually, including the "sins of his youth" (Psalm 25:7). In almost every case, even when he was struggling in the beginning of the psalm, by the end he had figured it out and was praising God. Psalm 88, said to be written by the sons of Korah, is the only one that doesn't follow this pattern. It starts out bad and gets worse—like French movies! The last sentence (verse 18) says: "the darkness is my closest friend." I hope that on a day when his perspective was clearer that the writer worked through it and soon wrote a more positive psalm!

In a preceding chapter I mentioned about the articles currently being published which explain the need to write out your feelings in order to handle them well. That is not a novel idea. David did it centuries and centuries ago. Why do you think Paul wrote about his persecution of the church as much as he did in the way that he did? Surely a part of it was his trying to remain open about an area of his life that was so horrifying for him to contemplate. Openness is not just a good idea; it is vital if we are going to get our insides lined up right. And writing is one of the very best ways not only to work through the past, but also to manage the present.

Obviously, Paul's statement in Philippians 3:13 about forgetting the past was never intended to be inclusive of past blessings. Gratitude for what God has done in the past also plays a vital role in dealing with the present and the future. In Philippians 4:6, Paul wrote these words: "Do not be anxious about anything, but in everything, by prayer and petition, with thanksgiving, present your requests to God." One part of the cure for anxiety about the future is thankfulness, which means that we pay the past a visit to some extent. The past blessings of God are invaluable in helping you deal with the challenge of the present. For example, what were we worrying about a year ago today? It's likely that we don't have a clue, which means that God brought us through whatever challenges we were facing then. Looking at the victories of the past and being thankful for them will alleviate the concerns of the present. God has always been faithful to us, hasn't he? Why begin to doubt now?

In this sense, the past is the key to the present. David had this principle in mind when he wrote, "I was young and now I am old, yet I have never seen the righteous forsaken or their children begging bread" (Psalm 37:25). If God has helped you through the challenges of the past, you can certainly trust him to do the same in the present and in the future.

As the old hymn says, "Count your many blessings, name them one by one, and it will surprise you what the Lord hath done." Every time I try to count all of my blessings from birth forward, as I did the morning that I wrote this chapter, I am surprised and amazed and very, very grateful. I appreciate so much of what makes up my past, minus the sins. The words God spoke concerning Jeremiah are to one extent or another true of all disciples:

> "Before I formed you in the womb I knew you, before you were born I set you apart; I appointed you as a prophet to the nations" (Jeremiah 1:5).

He does have a plan for each of us, to prosper and not to harm us.

If you have unfinished business in the past, work it through as quickly as possible, and then move on. In this way the past will come to hold only the good memories of the blessings of God. Looking back on our lives and seeing God's designs all over the landscape is a faith-building and gratitude-building exercise. Learn from your past, repent of past sins (but you have already done that, right?), be extremely grateful for the blessings, and by them, be moved to serve God as never before.

Growing in Gratitude

Do you think that anything from your past is having a significant impact on your present? (If no, praise God; if yes, get help and get open.)

Have you ever written out your prayers or feelings in an attempt to better understand yourself? Try it this week.

Some time soon, plan to spend at least one long prayer time thanking God for every major blessing you can remember—from birth to the present.

10

Another Kind of Adoption

"I tell you the truth," Jesus replied, "no one who has left home or brothers or sisters or mother or father or children or fields for me and the gospel will fail to receive a hundred times as much in this present age (homes, brothers, sisters, mothers, children and fields—and with them, persecutions) and in the age to come, eternal life."

Mark 10:29-30

I needed to go to Philadelphia to help out an old friend. The church leader there, Walter Evans, asked me to speak to one of their ministry groups on Sunday, since I was going to be in town until the next day. We discussed where I was most needed and settled on the campus group. I was pleased, since my personal preference is always to speak to this group—I love their youthful idealism and sharp minds.

However, on that particular day, to be honest, speaking was more of an assignment than a passion, so I did not have high expectations for the service. Thankfully, God did. I was looking forward to seeing my daughter's husband, Jeff (whom we call our "son by marriage," not "son-in-law"), who was in town for a wedding. When I arrived, I learned that a group of the HOPE Youth Corps would also be in attendance.

The service began with enthusiastic singing. My heart started stirring. Thank God for singing. The welcome by the campus ministry leader followed. Although I did not know the brother well at all, I was most impressed and thought to myself, "This is an amazing introduction to a service. I need to steal it!" Then after some other passionate songs, a campus ministry intern began the communion message. As it turned out, he was one of the top college debate team members in the country, and he spoke *well*. I was moved even more. Thank God for young leaders! He then introduced a campus woman from North Carolina who was to share what the cross had done in her life. I was unprepared for what was about to happen.

As she came up to the microphone, her physical beauty was apparent. Soon her spiritual beauty would be. Something about her voice was unusual, and for a few moments I couldn't identify why. I had heard similar voice and pronunciation qualities before, and suddenly I realized that Kelly was deaf. She shared about how her physical father had rejected her because she was deaf and therefore imperfect. She went on to share how her stepfather had rejected her and forced Kelly's mom to choose between her older children from a previous relationship and him (she chose him). She described the heartache, heartbreak and rebellion fostered by such rejection. Toward the end, she shared her conversion experience and closed with a profound but sad statement: she could picture God as Creator, as Savior and even as Husband, but she could not picture him as Father. Her concept of a father was seriously damaged by her life experiences.

By this time, tears were spilling down my cheeks and down Jeff's as well. Most of those young people in the audience were brushing back tears. I quickly wrote down Mark 10:29-30 on a note to Kelly, and offered to "adopt" her as my daughter. God had really moved my heart, and then he used me to move many other hearts during the sermon that followed. The whole experience could only be called a "God thing." After the lesson Kelly gave me a big hug, and I sensed that God was going to use all of this to do some healing in her.

The idea of being a spiritual dad for young people did not have a welcome beginning in my mind and heart. I had moved to San Diego to lead the church there when I was forty-two years old. One of the young interns (now an evangelist in Florida) asked to talk to me after a staff meeting. He shared that he felt really close to me, almost like I was his dad, and then he asked if he could call me "Dad." I replied, "Absolutely not!" I rebelled at the idea of being seen as that old. When I shared the experience with Ron, one of the elders there, he gave me a much different perspective. He talked about how many young disciples either do not have living fathers or they have poor relationships with them. He thought that being a dad to them was one of the best roles we could have. In essence, I said that that was fine for him, but not for me! (He was a couple of years older.)

The years have shown me just how right he was. Being a dad to the church in Boston and to our churches in Europe is my finest role at this point in my life. Randy McKean emphasizes this role well for Theresa and me, and I often marvel at what the concept seems to do for people.

A few years back, Bryan and Renee (our "natural" children) gave me a ring for Christmas which displays the word "Dad." They understood that I was not just a dad to them, but to many others. They often ask us to "adopt" some of their friends who need the spiritual love of mom and dad figures. Mark 10 has become one of my favorite passages because it gets at the heart of love in the kingdom—family love, adoptive love.

After the Philadelphia experience, I received a card from Kelly, asking if she could visit us in Boston, if only for a dinner. She had taken the adoption thing seriously.

I make the offer on a widespread basis, and some take me up on it in a special way (no doubt those who need it most). Kelly is one of those. She seemed to sense what John the apostle sensed in his relationship with Jesus. He felt totally at ease reclining on Jesus' bosom (the literal translation of John 13:23) at the Passover meal. He described himself in the same verse as "the disciple whom Jesus loved." Do you really think Jesus loved him more than he loved the other disciples? I rather think that Jesus loved all of them more than any of them could come close to grasping. But I do think that John was best at accepting and internalizing Jesus' love. He perceived at a deeper level what kind of relationship was there for the taking. People like John and Kelly simply claim what is actually available and soak up the love as a result.

Kelly came to Boston for a few days, and we shared our story at a workshop for singles. She later visited again for a few days with her younger sister, hoping to influence her by showing her what love in the kingdom is all about. Kelly has become a special daughter to me and Theresa and has found a lodging in our hearts and lives that will outlast this life. Kingdom relationships are closer than mere physical relationships. I may have trouble appreciating some things in the kingdom as much as I should, but the relationships I do understand and appreciate.

I, like untold numbers of others, am the product of a dysfunctional family. When I was younger, I looked for love "in all the wrong places," as the song says, but now I have discovered the true love of the family of God. He has granted me the high honor of being a dad to his family, and Theresa a mom. And the reason for this is that others might feel his love through us, and through every disciple, as we come to understand what his family is to be to the world and to one another. Then we will be able to lavish on others what he has lavished on us.

If we are not filled to overflowing with gratitude for the family of God, we simply have missed the essence of the gospel. Figure it out, for within these relationships are housed some of the most unbelievable blessings which will ever be known to mankind on this side of eternity.

> Then he looked at those seated in a circle around him and said, "Here are my mother and my brothers! Whoever does God's will is my brother and sister and mother." (Mark 3:34-35)

Growing in Gratitude

Are you generally thankful for relationships in the kingdom, or critical about them?

What can you do, practically, to build the concept of family love in your personal relationships and in your ministry group? List some ideas.

Think through the relationships that the two apostles John and Judas had with Jesus. What in the two men caused the vast differences? Use scriptures in your answer.

11

It Is So Hard—but I Love It!

Consider it pure joy, my brothers, whenever you face trials of many kinds, because you know that the testing of your faith develops perseverance. Perseverance must finish its work so that you may be mature and complete, not lacking anything.

James 1:2-4

A week before writing this, I saw a young sister for the first time since her recent marriage. I asked how marriage was, and with a beaming face, she said, "It is *so* hard—but I love it!" Not everyone feels so positively about those early marriage adjustments. As someone said, the hardest year of a good marriage is the first one, and the hardest year of a bad marriage is the last one, because in this case the people don't make the adjustments. John Gray struck quite a chord with his *Men Are from Mars, Women Are from Venus* books and lectures. Men and women are different—*very* different—and those differences can be both intriguing and highly frustrating at the same time.

Of course, James did not appear to have the trials of marriage specifically in mind when he wrote the above passage, but "trials of many kinds" would include them. Do you allow the trials in marriage and/or in life generally to rob you of your joy? Without doubt, the greatest test of our gratitude is how we view and react to those rather incessant trials.

Concerning marriage, I remember reading a book which described a way of differentiating between two common types of mind-sets toward personal discipline. Those who tended to be rigid and rules focused, the author called "Here comes the Judge." Those who tended to be the opposite, he named "Let it slide, Clyde." The former type think that being right on time is being late, and the latter think that being only ten minutes late is an accomplishment! The one cannot stand to have anything in the house out of place, while the other might not notice the presence of an elephant in the living room. Herein lies the challenge which the writer observed: most marriages seem to end up with one partner of each type.

In our marriage, Theresa is "Clyde," and she is married to the uptight old "Judge" (bless her heart!). Why does it often seem to work out that we marry people quite different from ourselves? I think it is because God is trying to work off the rough edges each of us has, and learning to live together forces the issue. Through the years, Theresa has become much more punctual and organized (often surpassing me in these areas), and I have become less (but not enough less) stringent about the details. The Clydes among us tend to be much more focused on people and relationships than the Judges. I pray that we learn to embrace the trials in marriage which come from our differences in personality and character, in order that we might enjoy the benefits it can produce.

One of the most remarkable differences in men and women is in our approach to communication. Men are usually quite succinct, while women relate most of the details. (How do they even remember all of that stuff?) Recently, a young evangelist friend came home after being in some long meetings, hoping for some romantic time with his wife, who had been in similar meetings with women leaders. She asked how his meetings went, and he said, "Great. How about yours?" No doubt he desired an equally brief answer, but he momentarily forgot that she was a woman! A "bump" quickly ensued, and it took more than two hours to be resolved and to finally have some romantic time together! By the time we heard about it, both husband and wife were amused, but you can bet that when it occurred, merriment was out of the question. I do think that both of them grew in their marriage as a result of the trial, which is what God expects to occur.

However, if we are to grow through trials, we must learn to view them correctly. How do you respond when life upsets your applecart? Some people immediately become hurt and angry. Anger is a response to hurt, but some of us are so conditioned in this response that we think the anger comes first. It doesn't. Other people try to act as if nothing bothers them, but inside it actually does. We all have to learn how to respond righteously (which includes not becoming angry), but denying disappointment or pain is not the response which works best. Still other people acknowledge the pain, but just continue to grind it out. Many of us turn to the "grin-and-bear-it," "this-too-shall-pass" mode when trials come our way. Any of these responses blocks us from the growth that God wants us to enjoy.

In the Garden of Gethsemane, Jesus expressed his emotional pain, but prayed long enough to resolve it by surrendering to the Father's will. One of the staggering passages about Jesus' response to trials is found in Hebrews 5:7-10.

> During the days of Jesus' life on earth, he offered up prayers and petitions with loud cries and tears to the one who could save him from death, and he was heard because of his reverent submission. Although he was a son, he learned obedience from what he

> suffered and, once made perfect, he became the
> source of eternal salvation for all who obey him and
> was designated by God to be high priest in the order
> of Melchizedek.

Here we find that loud cries and tears were a regular part of his prayer life, not just in Gethsemane ("during the *days*"). We also learn that having his prayers heard and answered did not mean the removal of the trials. Further, we see that he had to learn obedience through suffering, and that the obedience in suffering perfected him for his role as high priest. He was already sinless, but not perfect for his role until the trials had done their work. Every time I say or write that, it sounds almost blasphemous, but the text does affirm exactly this point.

If Jesus, the sinless, had to suffer to be perfected, we, the sinful, will need it even more. This is what we signed up for originally—to do whatever it takes to become more and more like Jesus, in order to represent him more effectively. Paul understood the principle perfectly, as Colossians 1:24 demonstrates:

> Now I rejoice in what was suffered for you, and I
> fill up in my flesh what is still lacking in regard to
> Christ's afflictions, for the sake of his body, which is
> the church.

Just as the suffering of Jesus on the cross became the attraction which drew all men to himself (John 12:32), our suffering has the same redemptive element inherent in it. Thus, trials both mature us and attract others at the same time.

However, if these purposes are to be accomplished, we must view and respond properly to the trials. As always, Jesus is our perfect example.

> When they hurled their insults at him, he did not retaliate; when he suffered, he made no threats. Instead, he entrusted himself to him who judges justly. He himself bore our sins in his body on the tree, so that we might die to sins and live for righteousness; by his wounds you have been healed. (1 Peter 2:23-24)

Peter gives us the challenge to respond the same way Jesus did: "But rejoice that you participate in the sufferings of Christ, so that you may be overjoyed when his glory is revealed" (1 Peter 4:13). I could quote many verses on the subject of being joyful and thankful in suffering, but the question is how well we are obeying them, isn't it?

Our daughter, Renee, has a plaque on her wall which reads: "It's not hard to be an angel, as long as no one ruffles your feathers." (Smile.) But our feathers get ruffled almost constantly, don't they? At the time of this writing, I have been staying in a little hotel in a beautiful lake setting working on this book for three full days. It is about as quiet and peaceful as any place I've ever stayed (if you don't count those loudmouth frogs I mentioned in the first chapter). But in less than forty-eight hours, this little respite will be history, and I will have reentered life as it is. I have made myself a mental note to be very careful about such reentries. If I am not on guard, coming down from the mountaintop to the valley of reality can be a hazardous experience for me and for those closest to me! Away from this serene spot there will be plenty of situations that will ruffle my feathers. Each will be a challenge, but also an opportunity to show gratitude even in the trials.

Well, what is the answer for you and me, as we seek to consistently handle our trials righteously? Good question. The answer, as always with God, is very simple but not very easy. It takes surrender to his will in our lives and the certain conviction that nothing happens by accident. Trying to gain heaven's perspective in every situation, through much prayer and meditating on the Word, is the goal. Even when we cannot figure out what God could possibly be doing, a childlike trust is the only response.

We are on this earth for a very limited time, and how we live determines our eternity. The question we ought to be asking when problems arise is not, "Why me?"; it is, "Why not me?" Heaven is the goal, and it won't be long in coming. With that in view, how much could our difficulties in life really weigh on the scales of eternity? It is, after all, a matter of spiritual comprehension and focus. Paul, in probably my favorite passage in the entire Bible, put it all together as only he could. If we can get his heart here, we can say of the Christian life, "It is so hard, but I love it!"

> Therefore we do not lose heart. Though outwardly we are wasting away, yet inwardly we are being renewed day by day. For our light and momentary troubles are achieving for us an eternal glory that far outweighs them all. So we fix our eyes not on what is seen, but on what is unseen. For what is seen is temporary, but what is unseen is eternal. (2 Corinthians 4:16-18)

Growing in Gratitude

What is your normal heart response to life's challenges and difficulties?

What types of qualities in other people tend to exasperate you? List them. What do you think God wants you to learn from each of these?

Which lessons from 2 Corinthians 4:16-18 can help you to respond to trials more righteously?

12

Is Your Job Sacred or Secular?

> Whatever you do, work at it with all your heart,
> as working for the Lord, not for men, since you
> know that you will receive an inheritance from
> the Lord as a reward. It is the Lord Christ you
> are serving.
>
> Colossians 3:23-24

The average adult spends a large percentage of his or her waking hours on the job, especially when you count preparation and travel time. It should be pretty obvious that having an attitude characterized by gratitude is going to be fairly difficult if we do not have a positive view of our jobs. Not all of us are going to have what we think is the job of our dreams, which means that we are going to need help from above to be happy and content with how we make our living. What does the Bible say about how to view our work?

The above passage, amazingly enough, is preceded by these words:

> Slaves, obey your earthly masters in everything;
> and do it, not only when their eye is on you and to
> win their favor, but with sincerity of heart and
> reverence for the Lord. (Colossians 3:22)

Now, whatever your job, I would imagine it is far better than the job of a slave. (You should be feeling more grateful already!) Yet, God expected even a slave to be happy with his lot in life. How could that be possible? The slave had to view his work as service to Christ, rather than simply to his earthly master, and he had to serve with sincerity of heart and reverence for the Lord. A few verses earlier, Paul had written:

> And whatever you do, whether in word or deed, do it all in the name of the Lord Jesus, giving thanks to God the Father through him. (Colossians 3:17)

Perhaps you are beginning to understand why the title of this chapter raises the question it does about the sacred and secular. (If not, I believe you will before we are finished with it.)

> Therefore, I urge you, brothers, in view of God's mercy, to offer your bodies as living sacrifices, holy and pleasing to God—this is your spiritual act of worship. (Romans 12:1)

This is another helpful passage. The bottom line of Paul's comments here is that all of life is to be viewed as worship to God, which would include the time spent on a job. Worship is not confined to congregational assemblies a few times a week, nor is it only during those assemblies plus our quiet times individually. Worship is a "24/7" issue—being God's disciples seven days a week, twenty-four hours a day. I'm not seeing much room for the secular, are you?

Sometimes I hear the statement that a person has left the "full-time ministry" and has taken a "secular" job. Of course, we all understand the facts being communicated, but do we understand the impression being left? I doubt it, or we would be using different terminology—better terminology, Biblical terminology. Personally, I am very concerned about how we describe such things, because I know that impressions can be left which are both misleading and hurtful.

For example, the phrase "ministry staff" (or even "full-time ministry staff") is descriptive and helpful, but the phrase "full-time ministry" alone is not. The latter term, which is a favorite with many of us (and for that reason, will not be given up easily!), implies that people who are not on the church staff are not in the ministry. If that is what we really believe, then we should not be preaching that passages like 2 Corinthians 5:18 ("the ministry of reconciliation") apply to every disciple.

The word "ministry" is a general word meaning "service." Applied specifically, it certainly can denote a ministry in the way we usually think of it, such as apostolic ministry (Acts 1:25), Paul's ministry as an apostle (Romans 11:13) or

Timothy's ministry as an evangelist (2 Timothy 4:5). But the word itself does not imply church-supported ministry, as we universally seem to apply it. Without doubt, the addition of "full-time" to the equation ushers in a conflict with the passages already quoted earlier. We are all full-time if we are disciples, plain and simple, whether supported by the church on staff or supported by our jobs.

What about the secular/sacred distinction? Here is what the dictionary says about the word "secular": "of or pertaining to worldly things or to things that are not regarded as religious, spiritual or sacred." Does this definition square with the passages already quoted in this chapter? No. Does it really matter? Probably not if you happen to be on the church staff, and probably so if you are not.

In a previous book, *Revolution: The World Changing Church in the Book of Acts*, I included a section in Chapter 8 entitled "Time for the Little People," which was about the widow, Dorcas. I pointed out that God saw fit to include more about her in the history book of the early church than about most of the apostles. (This also serves as evidence for inspiration, for men on their own would hardly leave out the exploits of their most prominent leaders.) My reason for including that section (besides the fact that God included it in Acts) was to

encourage those whose gifts and roles are not as obvious or glamorous as those of us who find ourselves in
the "up-front" roles. No child of the King of Kings should
feel like a second-class citizen! Since the book came out,
it has been interesting to note how many people in talking to me have referred to themselves as the "little
people." Even when accompanied by humor, their statements reveal something about their image of themselves
in the kingdom. And if terminology contributes to such
feelings, I am going to change mine and encourage others to do the same.

Everyone has gifts from God, be they genetic or envi-
ronmental in nature. We are born with some special tal-
ents or capabilities, and our environments have served to
help develop them. All of the gifts are to be used for the
purpose of serving others and not for serving ourselves
in some way. The gifts of the *whole* body of Christ reveal
Christ. A comparison of Colossians 2:9 with Ephesians
1:22-23 shows that just as Christ revealed the fullness of
God, the church reveals the fullness of *Christ!* Therefore,
leaving out part of the gifts diminishes our representation
and manifestation of Jesus Christ.

In Romans 12:6-8, one listing of such gifts, we find the
following: prophesying, serving, teaching, encouraging,

contributing to the needs of others, leadership and showing mercy. Three of the seven are more prominent gifts by
definition (prophesying, teaching, leadership), and the other
four are not. Every disciple with every kind of gift should
freely exercise their gifts and feel great about doing it,
even if they are not on the church ministry staff. Another
listing of gifts, 1 Corinthians 12, is primarily devoted to
eliminating attitudes of superiority or inferiority toward one
another. We will never eliminate such attitudes (which are
often subtle and unspoken) unless we figure out all of
what causes them and eliminate those causes. And I am
convinced that terminology is one of those causes.

A person earning a living working in a hospital is God's
minister to those medical professionals in his workplace. A
person teaching in a public school is God's light to those
other educators. A factory worker may sweat it out in an
assembly line physically, but spiritually he is the Lord's
example of what spirituality in the workplace is all about,
and he may be the Lord's only mouthpiece for the non-
Christian workforce there. Since the rest of us cannot be in
contact with all of these people in these environments, we
had better hope that those who do work there understand
that they are ministers of reconciliation. And they had better see their jobs as something more than secular ones.

Mark this down and punctuate it with an exclamation
point: The kingdom of God needs more, and more pow-
erful, leaders on the church staff! Those who have the

gifts which qualify them for such roles must have the ambition to serve in these capacities, for God has so equipped them. Woe unto us—and to them—when those who could serve powerfully in these roles are not motivated to desire them. Having more great leaders in church-supported staff roles is one of our most dire needs in the kingdom at this present time. Hence, we understand the renewed efforts to convert and raise up leaders in our campus ministries. It takes at least three things to serve in this way: leadership gifts from God's Spirit, a spiritual heart, and faith. If you have these, according to those leaders in your life who know you best, you should go after being on the staff with all of your energies. I love being supported by the church to do what I love doing. I would never want to be doing anything else, and I am deeply grateful to God and to all who support me financially, spiritually and emotionally.

However, I do not want any of those who provide my financial support to feel inferior to me or to ever feel like second-class citizens. Because of my somewhat prominent role, some tell me that I am their hero. I appreciate the encouragement and pray that God will help me to be more deserving of their esteem. Let me tell you who some of my special heroes are (in *addition* to the more influential ministry leaders on staff who are also close friends): the young interns on staff, who make many mistakes of inexperience and are discipled accordingly; those who are not church supported, but who lead groups of disciples in spite of many other responsibilities in life; the single moms, who have to fight for enough money to feed their kids and enough faith to keep going when their energy is totally depleted; those whose mates are not disciples, who have to deal with problems I cannot fully appreciate; those with physical challenges, who have to overcome the obstacles which we able-bodied folk do not comprehend; and many more who work behind the scenes and are unsung heroes.

In a word, my heroes are disciples who are doing what God has called them to do, regardless of leadership, ability or energy levels. We are one body, and every member is important to God and to the rest of us. Whatever else may be said, our spot on planet Earth is a sacred spot, not a secular one. Thank God for that!

Growing in Gratitude

What in this chapter struck the most emotional chords in you, positive or negative? Write it down.

What attitudes about the importance of yourself and others most need adjustment?

Do you often feel like a second class citizen in the kingdom, and if so, why? (It may be that your own attitude needs adjusting.)

13

Here I Raise My Ebenezer

Then Samuel took a stone and set it up between Mizpah and Shen. He named it Ebenezer, saying, "Thus far has the Lord helped us."

1 Samuel 7:12

As a young boy, I often heard a hymn sung in our church with this phrase in it: "Here I raise my Ebenezer." For many years, I had no idea what that meant, but it surely sounded strange! The stone described in 1 Samuel 7 was a stone of thanksgiving to God, meaning literally, "stone of help." The name came from a site near Aphek where the Israelites camped before they fought in battle against the Philistines (1 Samuel 4:1). During the second of two battles in the area, the Philistines captured the ark of the covenant. In a later battle, God intervened with a miraculous storm, allowing the Israelites to rout the Philistines and to recover the ark. It was at this time that Samuel erected the monument to which he gave the name Ebenezer.

Stones of remembrance were not new to the Israelites. When they crossed the Jordan River at the end of the wilderness wandering period, God had them set up a memorial of twelve stones, one for each tribe.

He said to the Israelites, "In the future when your descendants ask their fathers, 'What do these stones mean?' tell them, 'Israel crossed the Jordan on dry ground.'" (Joshua 4:21-22).

It is not hard to picture Jewish fathers squatting by those stones with their young children, describing the deliverance of their ancestors into their new homeland. I'm sure little hearts pounded rapidly as they heard stories which stretched their imaginations and enlarged their conception of the God of their fathers. Like them, we all need those landmark times etched in our memories to remind us of what God has done in our lives.

Last summer, as is our custom, Theresa and I went to Hawaii for vacation in order to visit our son Bryan, his wife, Joy, and our new grandson, Bryce (Bryce *Gordon*, by the way!). Early the next morning after arriving, I went on a prayer walk in Kapialoni Park at the end of Waikiki Beach, a location which held many memories for me.

As I prayed, I thought back to a Sunday morning six years earlier. The Oahu church celebrated its third year of existence with a special service on Father's Day, under a tent erected for that purpose in the park. I was privileged to be the guest speaker for the invitation service. As I recall, the attendance was more than one thousand, which was quite impressive for a group that started three years earlier with twenty-one disciples (including our son). It should have been a mountaintop experience for me, but in truth, it was not.

Both of our children had faced some spiritual challenges during that period of time, and I was worried about how they were ultimately going to do. When Theresa and I first began to be discipled in our marriage and family, Bryan was nearly twenty and Renee nearly sixteen. We made a lot of mistakes before that time, and the traditional churches we were in for many years added to the problems. But once in Boston, we were trying hard to learn, change and help our children to do the same. Frankly, it was a scary time for us as parents. Those fortunate enough to raise their children in a discipling church from infancy cannot really grasp what a blessing it is, nor can they understand fully what a challenge it is to miss out on such help in those early, formative years of your children's lives. By that Sunday morning in the park, we had made progress, but in my mind, the children were not out of the woods yet.

I remember preaching what I thought was a good sermon on paper, but my heart was unsettled. I felt somewhat hypocritical, as all preachers do at times, when we must preach God's ideals even though we feel we are falling far too short of them. At times like this, I simply pray that God will help me to repent and get back on track, but that he will use me and the lesson to help the people and accomplish his purposes (in spite of me). Thankfully, that particular morning he did exactly that.

In subsequent years, I met several disciples whose first visit to the church was that Sunday morning. One was a young man whose father refused to go to church with his family on Father's Day In anger, just to spite his father, he decided to attend the Oahu Church of Christ. His heart was really moved by the service, and before long, he was a disciple of Jesus and later was added to the ministry staff. Other conversion stories tracing back to that service are also very heartwarming. So when I say that this park held many memories for me, you can now better understand what I mean.

Last summer during that prayer walk, I thought back through those six years which had passed. Both of our children have matured excellently, have married wonderful mates who are absolutely tailor-made for them by God, and they are all doing very well as disciples. On top of those blessings is the little bundle of joy named Bryce, our first grandchild. And here we were vacationing in one of our favorite places on earth! About the time all of these things were beginning to hit my emotions, I glanced to my left and saw a stone that had been made into a monument of some type. I walked over to it, placed my hands on it, and looked over to the spot at the edge of the park where the tent had stood six years earlier. I broke

down and wept—wept for joy, amazed at what God had
done and how faithful to our family he had been. I thought
back to Samuel and the Ebenezer stone, and said to God,
"Thus far has the Lord helped us."

Disciples need special memories and reminders of
those memories. I have several small stones in my office
with dates on them, marking definitive prayer and decision times in my life when God enabled me to successfully jump a significant hurdle. I have albums of pictures
which remind me of spiritual times when God poured
out his love into my heart through the Holy Spirit (Romans 5:5). I have several file folders stuffed with printed
memorabilia describing the Lord's help in my life and in
that of my family. So many special events are recorded
on these "stones of remembrance"—the births of children,
the weddings of family and close friends, graduations,
birthdays and other such occasions, baptisms of those
who became a part of my heart as we shared the Word
together, celebration dinners commemorating these
events—and the list could go on and on.

Life seems to go by very fast—and very slowly. The
slow part particularly happens to disciples, because we
pack in so many things in a year's time. I make it a practice
to spend several days of each new year recounting the

events of the previous year. I keep very good calendars on my computer which allow me to do some detailed thanksgiving for what God has done with me and mine. These times are often accompanied by tears, because life with him is so very full and meaningful. Thinking back through the past eleven years in Boston makes me wonder how all of it could have possibly taken place.

Recently, on May 14, 1999, my heart filled to overflowing with memories as I thought back ten years to the same date in 1989. Renee had just turned seventeen two days earlier, and we were gathered on Sunday in the historic Boston Garden with the Boston Church of Christ. Kip McKean appointed me an elder and an evangelist, and Theresa was appointed as a women's counselor (in the terminology of the time). Bryan was on stage as a part of the church planting to Honolulu, joined by six other mission teams to be sent out the same day. It was truly incredible to witness such things!

After the service, Bryan and another member of the Hawaii team, David Hooper, packed the team leaders' car with their belongings and drove off into the sunset in the direction of California (the Robys' car was shipped over to Honolulu from there). Bryan finished college in Hawaii, met his wife there and now runs his own successful business there. Life has never been the same for any of us. A couple of years later, Renee left Boston as well, leaving us with not only an empty nest, but a pretty empty tree, as they now lived in other "forests."

Yes, time goes by slowly if we are filling our lives with God, because he packs an amazing amount of living into each of our years. But time goes by fast in other ways. As we disciple young parents about raising their children, Theresa often mentions some situation from our children's lives when they were young. I marvel that she can remember as many of the specifics as she does, for to me, those years seem so long ago and seemed like they sped by so fast. What happened to all of those years? Job understood the question, although he lived 140 years after his calamity (Job 42:16).

> "My days are swifter than a weaver's shuttle...." (Job 7:6)

> "My days are swifter than a runner....
>   They skim past like boats of papyrus,
>   like eagles swooping down on their prey."
> (Job 9:25-26)

> "Man born of woman
>   is of few days...
> He springs up like a flower and withers away;
>   like a fleeting shadow, he does not endure."
> (Job 14:1-2)

Life is too short not to make memories and then to regularly reflect on them with thankful hearts.

Memories. Precious memories. Another old hymn with that title describes God's faithfulness in our lives and goes on to refer to the work of "unseen angels from above." Life is being woven by God one day at a time into his own design, which only he knows. We fight the spiritual battle, sometimes feeling victorious and sometimes feeling defeated by our own weak flesh; at times seeing his mighty hand clearly and at other times wondering if he has forsaken us. But through it all, he is in control, working out his will. There is some good theology in the old songs. Truly "God moves in a mysterious way, his wonders to perform."

As Paul was striving to portray God's providential and mysterious work on man's behalf, he penned these immortal words: "Oh, the depth of the riches of the wisdom and knowledge of God! How unsearchable his judgments, and his paths beyond tracing out!" (Romans 11:33). As we look back at those paths of our lives which have become clearer with the passage of time, let us often state, "Here I raise my Ebenezer. 'Thus far has the Lord helped us.'"

Growing in Gratitude

Take the time to make a list of the high points in your life, and offer a long prayer of thanksgiving for them.

Analyze the list, and figure out the common elements that make them so special.

What have you learned about yourself from the above exercises?

14

Day-Tight Compartments

"Therefore do not worry about tomorrow, for tomorrow will worry about itself. Each day has enough trouble of its own."

Matthew 6:34

*S*ome things about life just feel strange. I would put death in that category. Just before writing this chapter I received a call from a very dear friend who called to tell me that his mother had just died. She had been ill for a long time, so death was neither sudden nor unexpected. But even then, death is a strange phenomenon. Someone we have known all of our life is gone, and we will never see them again—at least not in this world.

The sentence of death is on us and on everyone we know. All of us are going to have times like my friend who had just lost his mother. And one day someone is going to make that call about you and about me.

This a fairly heavy way to start off a chapter. However, it is reality, so we might just as well deal with it. In a sense, no matter how well things are going at any given point, such difficult times are bound to come for us all. How can we face such stark realities victoriously?

The words of Jesus in Matthew 6:34 are about as practical as any in the Bible. In essence, he tells us to live in day-tight compartments, focusing on today, rather than worrying about tomorrow. Tomorrow will arrive soon enough, with or without our being anxious about it. Just live in today for today. Since any time we have is a gift, we should be drinking deeply of the nectar of life, rather than focusing on how much might be left in the glass. This we cannot know, and for this we should be thankful. What if you knew the date of your last day? What would that do to you in the interim? Not much good, I suspect. It's better not to know and to just live one day at a time, as Jesus said.

However, to be candid with you, the aging issue is not easy for me. I still feel like a young guy inside, but my "outside" is going downhill. Paul described it with some tough words in 2 Corinthians 4:16, when he wrote that outwardly we are "wasting away." Sometimes I look at people out in public places who are older than I am and wonder if that is the next stage for me. If the culture watchers are correct, the Baby Boomers have difficulty accepting that they are aging and admitting that they are old. I am just a bit older than those who are normally put in that group, but my mind-set is similar on many points, including the way I view the aging process. All of us are going to have to learn how to apply Jesus' admonition of living one day at a time, or else life is not going to be much fun in our later years.

Several years back, I was visiting my mother when she still lived where I grew up. My uncle, her oldest sibling, and his wife came from a nearby town to see us. I was amazed at how youthful both he and his wife seemed in how they dressed and in just how they carried themselves. Thinking about my mother's age at the time, I knew that they had to be up there in years, but it didn't show much. I finally asked him how old they were, and he said that he was seventy-eight and my aunt was seventy-five. Not many their age are that youthful in attitude and action! We talked golf for awhile, and I asked if he wanted to drive back over for a game. He said yes, and we worked out the details. The day we teed off began as a hot, muggy Louisiana summer morning and got worse. Although he actually wanted to walk, I suggested that we ride in a cart, since my ankle had been bothering me.

We played eighteen holes, after which I asked if he might want to play more. He said, "Sure, let's play!" I thought that we would stop for lunch and some rest, but he wanted to keep going. After nine more holes, I assumed we would stop at that point. I was tired, and I thought surely he would be. But he said, "Let's go ahead and play the back nine." We ended up playing thirty-six holes of golf in that energy-draining weather, leaving me absolutely exhausted at the end of the day! I was so tired that I couldn't use any club in my bag to hit much past 150 yards, but on the thirty-sixth hole, Unk hit a long iron shot over a water hazard onto the green. As we were riding back to the club-house, he said, "Do you think you will tell anyone that a seventy-eight-year-old beat you on both rounds of golf?"

I said, "Yes, I'm going to tell them that he is my uncle and we share the same gene pool!"

I was fired up that he did beat me. I was most en-couraged to see someone his age who acted and played golf like someone decades younger. He knew how to fill each day with something besides worry about when the other shoe was going to fall. I even asked him about his sex life at seventy-eight (how often do you have an op-portunity to ask such a question?!), and his answer was quite encouraging!

The lesson here is that we can focus on today and remain vibrant, regardless of our age. The story of Caleb in the Old Testament is there for a reason (Numbers 14, Joshua 14). In the New Testament, Paul was one who became more and more intense as he aged. I am not going to allow myself to be put out to pasture as long as I can walk and talk, but the only way to accomplish this is to live in those day-tight compartments.

The most important factor in remaining effective and thankful as we do get older is to stay busy doing things that matter to God. Idleness is the devil's workshop, as the old saying goes, and it is also the mind's enemy. Too much thinking about ourselves becomes navel-gazing, which is unproductive at best and debilitating at worst. The woman of noble character in Proverbs 31 was busy from dawn to dusk, which contributed to her ability to "laugh at the days to come" (Proverbs 31:25). (It should be obvious that staying busy does not nullify the need to deal righteously with emotions or to do needed planning for the future.) In a similar vein, the writer of Ecclesiastes 5:19-20 wrote:

> Moreover, when God gives any man wealth and possessions, and enables him to enjoy them, to accept his lot and be happy in his work—this is a gift of God. He seldom reflects on the days of his life, because God keeps him occupied with gladness of heart.

Accepting our lots in life and deciding to be happy in our work go a long way toward helping us to live each day to the full, without thought of what tomorrow will bring.

I asked a very spiritual friend who is a few years older than I if he ever worried about aging and death. His answer was classic. "No," he said, "because I would be ungrateful for all of the blessings God has given me if I did." Great point.

I remember standing outside the men's dorm when I was in college and saying aloud that if I were to die then, I would have no complaints, since my life up to that point had been so good. Looking back, that was a very scary statement, for at that time I was not trying to live for God in any way. However, somehow I appreciated my life and realized that I had been blessed with happiness in many ways. Add thirty-six years to those twenty (the age at which I made that statement) and factor in the tremendous spiritual blessings I have since received as a lover of God, and the goodness of God becomes overwhelming. If ever I felt that dying would be fine in light of all that I have been able to do and enjoy, it should be now.

The day that I wrote this, I took a very long prayer walk around the little French lake where I am writing and did nothing but thank God for his blessings. I started with my birth and prayed through every stage of my fifty-six years that I could remember. I thought of events I had been able to enjoy, and there were many, many of them. It was fun to grow up as a Ferguson kid in Louisiana. I thanked God for the people who had somehow shaped in a good way who I became. I recalled Aunt Nora asking me as a boy of five if I was going to be a preacher when I grew up. My answer was yes, although I forgot the incident until after I became a preacher. A little seed was planted by God through an old lady. I remembered teachers who changed my destiny by seeing far more in me than I saw in myself, especially Mrs. Carter, Mrs. Teacle, Mr. Renfro and Mr. Simmons (who recently died just before his eightieth birthday).

If "every good and perfect gift is from above" (James 1:17), then all of those people were somehow God's gift to my life. I thanked God for dozens and dozens of key people who were placed in my path to shape me as a person and, in sometimes mysterious ways, to lead me to himself. I particularly thanked God for all of those spiritual friends and leaders who have loved me—when I was lovable and when I was not. I prayed most gratefully about falling in love with Theresa, getting married, having Bryan and Renee, seeing them marry the loves of their lives, Joy and Jeff, and seeing my grandson Bryce for the first time. I thought of the joy of having relatives in the kingdom, whose hearts have encouraged me more than mine has them.

And I think especially of the stilled form of the One who gave his last breath on a cross that all of this might be mine. Where would I be without him?

The tears roll down my cheeks as I write these words, for once again I am overwhelmed by the goodness of a God who blesses so abundantly in spite of what I have not been that I could have been. Yet once more, his kindness leads me to repentance (Romans 2:4).

Day-tight compartments? Yes, one after the other until there are no more, and then on to a very different kind of compartment where the day will never end. And there we shall bask in the love of God while the ages roll on, world without end. It has been well said: Yesterday is history; tomorrow is a mystery; but today is a gift from God, which is why we call it the *present!* Thank you, Father.

Growing in Gratitude

What percentage of your thought life focuses on past regrets and future worries?

Are thoughts of aging and death common to you, or uncommon? Give thought to why in either case.

What decisions about gratitude have you been prompted to make by reading this chapter?

15

Is This All There Is?

But whatever was to my profit I now consider loss
for the sake of Christ.

Philippians 3:7

*I*s this all there is to life? Good question, isn't it? I pity
those who never ask it, for they are seriously missing an
inner spiritual motivation to discover the real meaning of
life. Pascal said long ago that each of us is filled with a
God-shaped void that only he can fill by his presence.
Just as an adopted child longs to know his birth parents,
we long to know the Father of our spirits (Hebrews 12:9),
for we are made in his image for the purpose of having a
personal relationship with him. Of course, we need help
discovering all of that, but the search begins with the
question, *Is this all there is?*

Most of the physical pursuits of life discussed in the
book of Ecclesiastes are substitutes for what we really
need—a relationship with God. These pursuits are simply
misguided attempts to fill the void within, attempts which
will forever be doomed to failure. Hopefully you will identify with, and learn from, an account of my own search
for the answer to this central question of life. I suspect

that most of us have much in common as we grapple with the meaning of our lives.

It was thirty years ago when this question first pierced my heart and my consciousness. I will never forget the day nor the feeling. At age twenty-five, I stood on the pier of my fishing camp with my nice turquoise fiberglass bass boat tied alongside. My fishing partner for the day had already left, and I was standing on the pier, soaking in the satisfied feeling of having caught the limit of black bass that morning and enjoying the feeling of having such a good life. After all, my expectations in life had for the most part been met. The Great American Dream was pretty much a reality for me.

I had graduated from college with my wife and was about halfway through my master's degree. I was happily married to a beautiful, loving woman. We had a new baby boy—a healthy, happy, cutie-pie kid. We had bought a house within months of being married, and then traded up to a nicer one—three bedrooms, two baths, brick, on a large wooded lot with a nice fenced backyard. We had not only my bass boat and the fishing camp with a great waterfront and pier, but also a trailer camper and five acres of land in a restricted development on which to build our dream house. I had been successful at work, and the potential for advancement was within easy reach. What more could any twenty-five-year-old young man want?

But as I gazed out on that calm cypress-studded lake that mid-morning, the question pierced my innermost being, my soul: Is this all there is? To have achieved my dreams at such a young age was scary, especially when they really didn't satisfy at the deeper, almost imperceptible level. All I had to look forward to was more of the same for forty or fifty more years. Something about that did not seem right, and a gnawing emptiness pushed its way through the caverns of my heart and made itself known that day.

From then on, the pursuit of the spiritual began motivating me more than possessions or accomplishments. The transition from one mode of thinking to a very different one was not immediate nor complete, but it had begun. And it was destined to change the course of my future in a radical way, as the spiritual assumed a prominent position in my life. The thirty years since are now history, known by many who have known me and by those who have read my books.

When I was in my late thirties and preaching for a traditional church, I definitely asked the question again, which led me to do two things: to develop a personal walk with God (out of pure desperation) and to seek the movement of which I am now a part. From the point I found this movement, I generally have felt that I was living out my greatest dreams.

However, I later found myself asking a similar question even about my ministry in Boston: "Is something still missing?" I had been appointed an elder in 1989, as well as an evangelist, by one of my heroes, Kip McKean. Somehow, I did not find my complete answer in serving in these roles, as great as both are. Regrettably, my motivation for leading my ministry group waned, and, as a result, it became mediocre. While I can't blame anyone or anything for my own sin in this regard, still lingering in my mind was what I believe to be a legitimate concern regarding my fairly extensive Biblical training and teaching experience. Would I ever use these again in more in-depth ways that would have a broader impact? In the spring of 1993, God's answer became clear, and I was appointed a teacher, one of the now five who are recognized as kingdom teachers. In this role, I have been given the opportunity to teach on a much broader basis, train ministry staff, and write books for disciples, all of which has yielded an impact far beyond my imagination. God be praised!

But last summer, at age fifty-five, I found myself asking the same type of question about the soul's ultimate quest. Life has been far more than I could have asked or imagined. After years of searching for a church which was carrying out the dream planted in me primarily by Richard Hostetler, a preacher friend who influenced me greatly in my early years, I finally found it and became a part of it. I find myself one of those five kingdom teachers; a respected elder and author in the kingdom; a part of Randy McKean's top leadership group for his world sector; the husband of a wife who excels at loving people, especially me and the kids. I am the father of two grown children who are disciples very happily married to disciples with my firstborn now a new father himself, thus making me a grandfather. And yet the feeling and its accompanying question flooded my soul once again—is there yet more?

On several pivotal occasions, I have asked such questions and found an answer within the framework of the spiritual life somewhere. Each answer led me to another level—a good level, a satisfying level at the time—but only for a time, and then the question surfaced yet again. What remains?

Now comes the final answer to all these questions. When this answer is fully grasped the questions need no longer haunt us. The answer is in Philippians 3:7-11:

> But whatever was to my profit I now consider loss for the sake of Christ. What is more, I consider everything a loss compared to the surpassing greatness of knowing Christ Jesus my Lord, for whose sake I have lost all things. I consider them rubbish, that I may gain Christ and be found in him, not having a righteousness of my own that comes from the law, but that which is through faith in Christ—the righteousness that comes from God and is by faith. I want to know Christ and the power of his resurrection and the fellowship of sharing in his sufferings, becoming like him in his death, and so, somehow, to attain to the resurrection from the dead. (Philippians 3:7-11)

The answer? To be totally immersed in my relationship with God through Christ to the point that all other incomplete goals and motivations are engulfed in this one great quest. To know God in such a way and at such a level that all else pales into insignificance. When this level is reached, nothing else will matter—position, recognition, performance, respect or any other accolade from men. Further (and for me this is a biggie), the fear of death will lose its hold on my heart and absolutely disappear. Do I believe that such is possible? Absolutely—without a trace of doubt.

Therefore, I find myself excited about finding the answer to these age-old questions once more, but this time at a level that eliminates them from ever coming back to my heart again. I now embark on a lifetime quest, for whatever remaining years I may have. I feel quite settled about the pursuit, and quite grateful for the challenges emotionally and spiritually that prompted me to reach this ultimate stage of the search.

God, you being my Helper, this pursuit will I begin, and I will never turn from it until I draw my last breath, my soul departs this aging body and I see you for who you are. Thank you so very, very much for the answer. Now help me to grab on to it and to never let go, no matter how great the pain becomes that the pursuit requires. May I be able to feel deeply and state unequivocally the same sentiments expressed by your servant Paul long ago: "For to me, to live is Christ and to die is gain" (Philippians 1:21).

Growing in Gratitude

Have you ever asked a question similar to "Is this all there is to life?"? When?

How have you sought answers to this question, and what did you find out?

Where are you right now in reference to what this chapter calls the final level of such questions?

Thankful Books

*A*re you as thankful as you should be? Me neither. I wish that we were all much more naturally grateful than we are. Hopefully some of the ideas in the book will help us all to become those who are "overflowing with thankfulness" (Colossians 2:7), as we really should be. Beyond what has already been written, what can help us become characterized by gratitude?

Many of the New Testament passages about gratitude simply tell us to be thankful. This is not surprising, since thanksgiving is a part of prayer, and prayer is commanded. Everything in the Bible that is good for us is commanded. God does not just leave it up to the ebb and flow of our own wills and emotions to do what is right. He tells us to do it, for our own good. Therefore, the answer to becoming more grateful is in one sense very simple—just do it. If you focus much more on thankfulness in your prayer times and in your study times, then it will become a righteous habit (and righteous habits are excellent, as long as our hearts stay involved). We cannot simply wait for our attitudes to be perfect before we do what is right; in fact, doing what is right usually changes our attitudes if we desire deep down to experience such changes.

For sure, we need to make decisions about ways to add more thanksgiving to our daily times with God. One such way is to start a *Thankful Book*. Just recently, Theresa and I had a meal in Paris with an American couple living in Amsterdam. They have three children: two daughters, ages seven and five, and a son who is three. These little ones all have *Thankful Books* in which they draw pictures or write about what they are thankful for each day. Given their ages, drawing pictures is their most accessible way of depicting their gratitude. They do this just before going to bed every night. Can you imagine what eighteen years of this is going to do in their lives? Being thankful on a daily basis in this manner will likely have an amazing impact on the spiritual formation of their hearts. Parents—we need to learn something here, don't we?

Predictably, my wife has now started her own *Thank ful Book* and has encouraged other women to do the same. Whatever works for you is great, but we must all find something that does work. God is too good for us not to learn to express gratitude far better than most of us do. Take time to meditate on how you can practically develop that marvelous attitude of gratitude.

To give you a few ideas with which to begin, perhaps you could come up with seven areas of gratitude and incorporate one area into your prayers each day of the week. Or, you could begin each prayer time with a certain number of minutes spent in doing nothing but giving thanks. Further, you could categorize different types of people in your life from your early years to the present who have helped mold who you are, or for whom you are thankful for whatever reason. You could make other categories of physical blessings or family blessings or spiritual blessings, and divide them up for inclusion in your prayers at specific intervals. The main point here is that we must determine to make all parts of our prayers personal between us and God, especially our thanksgiving.

After hearing about *Thankful Books*, many of us will look longingly back to our childhood and wish that our parents had given us such guidance. Had they done this, we would be different adults today. Since something like that happened to too few of us, we need a concrete, well-planned approach to help us as "spiritual babes" learn to be more and more grateful to our perfect Father, the God of all grace. Let us begin by deepening our convictions and looking for the inspiration to act on these convictions. It is never too late to change. The presence of a grateful heart permeates everything we do and who we are. Be willing to pay any price required to develop it. Then you will enjoy daily a bit of heaven on earth. Let's do it, for the praise of his glory!

Who Are We?

Discipleship Publications International (DPI) began publishing in 1993. We are a nonprofit Christian publisher affiliated with the International Churches of Christ, committed to publishing and distributing materials that honor God, lift up Jesus Christ and show how his message practically applies to all areas of life. We have a deep conviction that no one changes life like Jesus and that the implementation of his teaching will revolutionize any life, any marriage, any family and any singles household.

Since our beginning we have published more than 75 titles; plus we have produced a number of important, spiritual audio products. More than one million volumes have been printed, and our works have been translated into more than a dozen languages—international is not just a part of our name! Our books are shipped regularly to every inhabited continent.

To see a more detailed description of our works, find us on the World Wide Web at www.dpibooks.com. You can order books by calling 1-888-DPI-BOOK twenty-four hours a day. From outside the US, call 781-937-3883, ext. 231 during Boston-area business hours.

We appreciate the hundreds of comments we have received from readers. We would love to hear from you. Here are other ways to get in touch:

Mail: DPI, One Merrill St., Woburn, MA 01801
E-mail: dpibooks@icoc.org

Find us on the
World Wide Web

www.dpibooks.com
1-888-DPI-BOOK
outside US: 781-937-3883 x231